Build Your Linux Firewall Mastery

Unlock the Power of IPtables, NFTables, and UFW

Written by, Lynne Kolestar

Table Of Contents

Part 1: Introduction to Linux Firewalls

Chapter 1: The Importance of Firewalls in Linux

Overview of Firewalls and Why They Matter

Firewalls are an essential component of network security, serving as the first line of defense between a system and external threats. In Linux environments, firewalls help monitor, filter, and control incoming and outgoing network traffic based on predefined security rules. Their primary function is to prevent unauthorized access to or from a private network while allowing legitimate communication to pass through.

In today's connected world, where cyberattacks are on the rise and data protection is of high concern for most businesses, a properly configured firewall is crucial for protecting sensitive data, ensuring service availability, and mitigating risks from malicious actors. For Linux-based servers, desktops, and IoT devices, firewalls play a critical role in maintaining the system's integrity, whether they are part of a small personal setup or a large-scale enterprise infrastructure. By regulating traffic flow and blocking suspicious activities, firewalls can thwart attempts such as Distributed Denial of Service (DDoS) attacks, port scanning, brute force login attempts, and unauthorized access to sensitive services.

Linux firewalls not only secure individual systems but also provide a means to enforce network policies across an entire infrastructure. Their flexibility and power, particularly with tools like IPtables, NFTables, and UFW, enable system administrators to fine-tune network access and protect mission-critical services from both external and internal threats.

Evolution of Linux Firewalls: From IPtables to NFTables

Linux firewalls have evolved significantly over the years, adapting to the
growing complexity of network infrastructures and the increasing sophistication of threats. Historically, IPtables has been the cornerstone of firewall management in Linux. Released in the late 1990s as part of the 2.4 Linux kernel, IPtables offered a robust, rule-based firewall system that allowed administrators to control network traffic at the packet level. Its architecture was built around tables, chains, and rules, which gave users the ability to filter, route, and modify network traffic with great flexibility.

However, as network architectures grew more complex, IPtables began to show its limitations. The configuration syntax became cumbersome for managing large sets of rules, and performance issues arose when handling higher traffic volumes. This led to the development of NFTables, which was introduced in the 3.13 Linux kernel as a more efficient and modern alternative to IPtables. NFTables is designed to replace both IPtables and IP6tables (for IPv6), streamlining firewall management by using a more concise syntax and providing improved performance, especially in high-throughput environments. It also offers better scalability, as it uses a single framework for managing both IPv4 and IPv6 traffic, NAT, and bridging rules, making it easier for system administrators to manage complex rulesets.

In comparison to IPtables, NFTables significantly reduces redundancy by eliminating the need for separate tools for IPv4 and IPv6, and its use of sets for rule optimization results in faster rule matching. NFTables also supports more advanced features like concatenated keys, dynamic sets, and atomic rule updates, giving administrators more control over complex scenarios while improving the overall performance of the firewall system.

A Comparison Between Hardware and Software Firewalls

Firewalls come in two primary forms: hardware firewalls and software firewalls, each with distinct advantages and limitations. In Linux environments, software firewalls like IPtables, NFTables, and UFW dominate, but it's important to understand where they fit in relation to hardware solutions.

Hardware firewalls are physical devices positioned at the

network perimeter, often integrated into routers or dedicated security appliances. They are designed to filter traffic before it reaches the internal network. These firewalls are generally more efficient for handling large volumes of traffic because they offload filtering tasks from individual machines. Hardware firewalls provide centralized control over the entire network, making them ideal for enterprises where traffic management at the edge is critical. They can effectively block unwanted traffic from reaching any devices within the protected network, providing protection at the network's ingress point.

However, hardware firewalls are typically more expensive, as they require dedicated, specialized hardware, which can represent a significant upfront cost, especially for small businesses or home users. Additionally, they may lack the granularity needed to protect individual servers or devices within the network. While hardware firewalls offer a broad layer of protection, their fixed level of configurability can make them less adaptable to the evolving security needs of a complex, multi-layered network environment. This often results in organizations supplementing hardware firewalls with software firewalls for more precise control.

In contrast, software firewalls like those implemented on Linux systems offer greater flexibility and can be customized to suit the security requirements of individual devices or services. A software firewall installed on a Linux machine can be fine-tuned to filter traffic based on specific ports, IP addresses, or protocols, allowing for much more granular control. While hardware firewalls protect the network as a whole, software firewalls add an extra layer of defense at the device level, ensuring that even if malicious traffic bypasses the hardware firewall, it can still be blocked locally.

Linux's software firewalls are also highly scalable. From a single home PC to an entire server farm, tools like IPtables and NFTables allow administrators to implement detailed security policies on a per-host basis. The flexibility and open-source nature of these firewalls allow for continuous updates and custom rules tailored to meet the specific needs of the user.

Ultimately, the choice between hardware and software firewalls—or a combination of both—depends on the size, complexity, and security needs of the network. In many cases, Linux administrators will use software firewalls alongside hardware firewalls to ensure comprehensive protection across all levels of the network.

Chapter 2: Networking Basics for Firewall Configuration

IP Addressing, Subnets, and Ports

Before diving into firewall configuration, it's important to understand how networks operate, particularly with concepts like IP addressing, subnets, and ports. These are the foundational elements that firewalls use to control and filter traffic.

Every device connected to a network, whether a local system or an internet-connected device, is identified by an IP address (Internet Protocol address). In IPv4, the address is composed of four sets of numbers, known as octets (e.g., 192.168.1.1), with each octet ranging
from 0 to 255. This results in an IPv4 address range from **0.0.0.0** to **255.255.255.255**. However, some portions of this address space are reserved for specific purposes, such as private networks or multicast addresses. For example, the address range 192.168.1.* is commonly used for private networks or intranets and you may have noticed this on your home router.

IPv4 (Internet Protocol version 4) is the most widely used protocol for assigning unique IP addresses to devices on a network. It provides a 32-bit address space, allowing for approximately 4.3 billion unique IP addresses, which are used to identify devices on the internet and within local networks. IPv4 is essential for routing data between devices by using these addresses, ensuring that information reaches the correct destination across complex networks. Despite the limited number of addresses available, IPv4 has been fundamental in supporting global internet connectivity for decades, providing the foundation for services ranging from websites and email to online gaming and cloud computing. However, as the number of internet-connected devices grows, IPv4's address space has become exhausted, leading to the gradual adoption of IPv6.

To address the growing demand for IP addresses, IPv6 was introduced, expanding the address space significantly. IPv6 uses a 128-bit address format, represented as eight groups of four hexadecimal digits, separated by colons (e.g., 2001:0db8:85a3:0000:0000:8a2e:0370:7334). Each group corresponds to 16 bits of the address, offering a vastly larger address pool. To simplify, IPv6 addresses can be abbreviated by omitting leading zeros within each group. Consecutive groups of zeros can also be replaced with a double colon (::) for readability, such as converting:

2001:0db8:85a3:0000:0000:8a2e:0370:7334
     to
2001:db8:85a3::8a2e:370:7334.

However, the double colon can only be used once in an address to prevent ambiguity.

The introduction of IPv6 resolves the limitations of IPv4's 32-bit address space, which could only support around 4 billion unique addresses. In contrast, IPv6's 128-bit address space supports an enormous 340 undecillion (3.4×10^{38}) addresses, providing ample capacity for the growing number of internet-connected devices.

IPv6 resolves the limitations of IPv4's 32-bit address space, which could only support around 4 billion unique addresses. In contrast, IPv6's 128-bit address space supports an enormous 340 undecillion (3.4×10^{38}) addresses, providing ample capacity for the growing number of internet-connected devices.

This vast address space is essential for the Internet of Things (IoT), where billions of devices, such as smart home products, sensors, and industrial machinery, need individual addresses. IPv6 also eliminates the need for complex address translation mechanisms like Network Address Translation (NAT), which are often required in IPv4. Additionally, IPv6 supports large-scale network infrastructure and mobile networks, ensuring end-to-end connectivity as users seamlessly access services across different networks.

The 128-bit addressing also allows for efficient subnetting, enabling large organizations or service providers to manage vast numbers of servers and routers. Designed to future-proof the internet, IPv6 ensures that the network can scale and evolve, overcoming IPv4's limitations and providing a nearly unlimited supply of addresses for the foreseeable future. This expansive addressing is crucial for next-generation networking and global internet expansion, especially in sectors like mobile networks, cloud computing, and smart cities.

IP addresses, whether in IPv4 or IPv6 format, are essential for routing traffic between devices and across networks, ensuring that data reaches the correct destination.

A subnet (short for subnetwork) is a logical subdivision of an IP network. Subnets help organize and optimize traffic flow within networks by grouping devices into smaller, manageable segments. They are defined by a subnet mask, which determines the range of IP addresses that belong to the subnet. For example, in a network with the IP address 192.168.1.0 and a subnet mask of 255.255.255.0, all devices within the 192.168.1.x range are considered part of the same subnet. Firewalls use subnetting to apply rules to specific ranges of IP addresses, allowing more granular control over network traffic.

Ports are another essential concept in networking and firewall configuration. A port is a logical endpoint for communication, allowing multiple services or applications to use the same IP address but different port numbers. For example, web traffic typically uses port 80 for HTTP or port 443 for HTTPS, while email servers use port 25 for SMTP. Firewalls regulate traffic by filtering data based on specific port numbers, either allowing or denying access to certain services.

Understanding IP addresses, subnets, and ports is fundamental to configuring a firewall because these are the key components firewalls use to define and enforce security rules.

TCP vs. UDP: Understanding Protocols

The Transmission Control Protocol (TCP) and User Datagram Protocol (UDP) are two of the most widely used protocols in network communication. While they both handle the transmission of data across networks, they do so in different ways, and this difference is crucial for configuring firewalls effectively.

TCP is a connection-oriented protocol, meaning it establishes a reliable connection between the sender and receiver before transmitting data, much like a handshake between two people before they begin to engage with each other. It ensures that data is sent in an orderly fashion, checks for errors, and resends lost packets if necessary. For example, web browsing, email, and file transfers typically use TCP because these applications require data integrity. TCP's reliability makes it ideal for applications where the completeness and accuracy of data are critical.

UDP, on the other hand, is a connectionless protocol. It sends data packets without establishing a dedicated connection and does not guarantee delivery. This makes UDP faster but less reliable than TCP, as it doesn't check for lost packets or errors. UDP is often used in real-time applications such as streaming, gaming, or video conferencing, where speed is more important than perfect accuracy.

From a firewall perspective, understanding the difference between TCP and UDP is vital for setting up proper rules. For example, if you're configuring a firewall for a web server, you'll need to allow traffic on TCP ports (e.g., 80 and 443). If you're setting up a streaming service, you might need to open specific UDP ports. Firewalls can filter traffic based on whether it's using TCP or UDP, giving administrators greater control over the types of connections allowed into or out of the network.

The Role of Packets and How Firewalls Filter Them

At the core of all network communications are packets—small units of data that are sent across networks. When data is transmitted, whether it's a file, email, or video stream, it is broken down into smaller pieces called packets, which are transmitted individually and then reassembled at the destination. Each packet contains both the data being sent and metadata, including information about the source and destination IP addresses, port numbers, and the protocol being used.

Firewalls work by inspecting these packets as they enter or leave the network. They filter packets based on a set of predefined rules, such as allowing packets from trusted IP addresses or blocking packets from suspicious sources. Firewalls examine the packet headers, which contain the essential information like source and destination IP addresses, port numbers, and protocol type, to determine whether the packet should be
allowed through or blocked.

There are different types of firewalls, including stateless and stateful firewalls, which handle packets in different ways. Stateless firewalls filter packets solely based on the predefined rules and do not keep track of the connection's state. For example, a stateless firewall might allow traffic from a specific IP address but won't remember whether that traffic is part of an ongoing connection.

Stateful firewalls, on the other hand, are more sophisticated. They monitor the state of active connections and make decisions based on the context of the traffic. For instance, a stateful firewall might allow a packet that's part of an established connection but block a packet if it comes unexpectedly from a new source.

Understanding how packets function and how firewalls filter them is critical when configuring firewall rules. Administrators can specify rules based on packet details, such as blocking packets from specific IP ranges, filtering based on port numbers, or even inspecting the protocol being used (TCP or UDP). With these controls, firewalls can effectively prevent malicious traffic from entering the network, while allowing legitimate communication to continue uninterrupted.

Chapter 3: Firewall Concepts and Terminology

Firewalls are a critical component in network security, acting as a barrier between trusted internal networks and potentially harmful external networks. This chapter introduces the core concepts and terminology associated with firewalls, including packet filtering, Network Address Translation (NAT), and the distinctions between stateful and stateless firewalls.

Packets, Filtering, and NAT (Network Address Translation)

At the heart of firewall functionality is packet filtering. Data transmitted across networks is divided into small units called packets, each containing both the data being sent and information about its origin and destination. A firewall inspects these packets to decide whether to allow or block them, based on predefined security rules.

Firewall rules are set up to filter packets by criteria such as:

Source IP address: The address from which the packet originates.

Destination IP address: The address where the packet is heading.

Port number: The specific service or application the packet is trying to communicate with (e.g., HTTP traffic typically uses port 80).

Protocol: The communication protocol being used, such as TCP or UDP.

These rules allow a firewall to either permit or deny traffic, effectively controlling what enters or exits the network.

Network Address Translation (NAT) is another important function commonly associated with firewalls. NAT allows multiple devices within a private network to share a single public IP address when accessing the internet. When a device on the private network sends a request to an external server, the firewall's NAT mechanism modifies the packet's source address, replacing it with the firewall's public IP. When the response arrives, the firewall translates the destination address back to the private address of the requesting device. This process helps to preserve the limited number of public IP addresses available and enhances security by hiding internal network details from the outside world.

Understanding Firewall Chains, Tables, and Rules

Firewall chains, tables, and rules are fundamental concepts in configuring and managing firewalls. A firewall operates by processing network traffic through a series of chains, where each chain consists of a set of rules that determine how packets should be handled. The most common chains are the Input chain, which handles traffic destined for the firewall itself, the Output chain, which processes traffic originating from the firewall, and the Forward chain, which deals with traffic being routed through the firewall to other networks. These chains are organized into tables, with the two primary tables being the filter table (which manages packet filtering rules) and the NAT table (which handles Network Address Translation). Rules within each chain are evaluated in sequence, and when a packet matches a rule, the firewall takes the specified action—such as allowing, blocking, or logging the packet. This structure allows network administrators to define precise traffic control policies, enhancing security and ensuring that only authorized traffic is allowed through the firewall.

To effectively manage traffic, firewalls organize their rules into structures known as chains, tables, and rules:

Chains: Chains are a sequence of rules that define how packets are processed. A typical firewall might have three main chains: **Input**, **Output**, and **Forward**.

Input chain: Handles packets destined for the firewall itself.

Output chain: Handles packets originating from the firewall.

Forward chain: Deals with packets being routed through the firewall to another network.

Tables: Firewalls group chains into tables, which organize rules for different types of traffic processing. The two primary tables are:

Filter table: The default table that handles packet filtering based on rules such as "allow" or "deny".

NAT table: Deals with address translation, ensuring that packets are correctly translated between private and public IP addresses.

Rules: Each chain is made up of individual rules, which define how packets should be handled. These rules are evaluated in sequence, with each packet being checked against the rules in the chain. If a packet matches a rule, the firewall takes the action specified in the rule (e.g., allow, block, or log the packet).

Stateful vs. Stateless Firewalls

Firewalls can be classified as stateful or stateless, and the distinction plays a key role in how they manage and filter traffic:

Stateful firewalls: These firewalls track the state of active connections. They remember the context of a session, including the source and destination of the traffic, as well as the type of connection. When a packet is received, the stateful firewall checks whether it is part of an established session or a new connection attempt. If it's part of an existing session, the firewall allows the packet to pass. This ability to track the state of a connection allows stateful firewalls to make more intelligent decisions about traffic, such as recognizing that a response packet corresponds to a legitimate outbound request. Stateful firewalls are more secure and efficient for handling complex traffic patterns.

Stateless firewalls: In contrast, stateless firewalls do not track the state of connections. Instead, they treat each packet individually, inspecting it based solely on the information contained in the packet (e.g., IP address, port, and protocol). Stateless firewalls are simpler and faster than stateful firewalls, but they are less secure because they do not consider the broader context of the traffic. As a result, stateless firewalls are typically used in simpler or less demanding environments where stateful inspection is unnecessary.

Part 2: Mastering IPtables

Chapter 4: Introduction to IPtables

History and Role of IPtables in Linux Systems

IPtables has been a core component of Linux firewall functionality since the 2.4 kernel version, replacing the older IPChains system. It serves as a user-space utility program for configuring the Netfilter framework within the Linux kernel, which is responsible for packet filtering, network address translation (NAT), and other network-related operations. In essence, IPtables acts as a gatekeeper, controlling the flow of network traffic into and out of a system based on specified rules. Over the years, IPtables has evolved to become one of the most widely used firewall solutions on Linux systems, offering administrators granular control over network traffic, security, and access control. It is often used to secure servers, prevent unauthorized access, implement NAT, and provide various forms of traffic filtering for both personal and enterprise networks.

Installing IPtables

Installing IPtables is typically straightforward on most Linux distributions. The installation process depends on the package manager of the distribution you're using.

On Debian/Ubuntu-based systems:

Update your package list and install IPtables using the following commands:

sudo apt update
sudo apt install iptables

On Red Hat/CentOS/Fedora-based systems:

On Red Hat-based distributions, you can install IPtables using yum or dnf (for newer Fedora versions):

sudo yum install iptables

Or on Fedora (using dnf):

sudo dnf install iptables

Configuring IPtables Rules

Once IPtables is installed, you can configure firewall rules through the command line by adding or removing rules.

For instance, to allow incoming HTTP traffic on port 80 (HTTP), you would add the following rule:

sudo iptables -A INPUT -p tcp --dport 80 -j ACCEPT

This command does the following:

-A INPUT: Appends a rule to the INPUT chain (for incoming traffic).

-p tcp: Specifies the protocol as TCP.

--dport 80: Matches traffic destined for port 80 (HTTP).

-j ACCEPT: Specifies that the matching traffic should be accepted.

Saving IPtables Rules

After you have configured IPtables, it is important to save the rules so that they persist after a reboot.

On Debian/Ubuntu-based systems:

You can save the current IPtables configuration with the iptables-save command:

sudo iptables-save > /etc/iptables/rules.v4

This saves the rules to the /etc/iptables/rules.v4 file. You can later modify or review this file as needed.

To make the rules persistent across reboots, the iptables-persistent package can be used, which ensures that the rules are automatically restored at boot.

To install iptables-persistent:

sudo apt-get install iptables-persistent

During the installation, you will be prompted to save the current rules. If you choose "Yes," the rules will be saved, and the system will automatically restore them during the boot process using iptables-restore.

Alternatively, you can manually restore the rules with the following command:

sudo iptables-restore < /etc/iptables/rules.v4

On Red Hat/CentOS/Fedora-based systems:

On Red Hat-based systems (such as CentOS or Fedora), IPtables rules are typically saved to the /etc/sysconfig/iptables file.

You can save the current IPtables configuration by running:

sudo service iptables save

This will store the rules in the /etc/sysconfig/iptables file. You can also manually edit this file if necessary.

To ensure that IPtables rules are restored on boot, you need to enable the iptables service:

sudo systemctl enable iptables

This will ensure that IPtables is loaded and the saved rules are applied when the system reboots.

Restoring IPtables Rules on Reboot

After saving the IPtables rules, the rules must be restored on system boot to ensure the firewall configuration persists.

On Debian/Ubuntu-based systems:

If you have installed iptables-persistent, the system will automatically restore the rules on boot.

However, if you are not using iptables-persistent and want to manually restore rules, you can add a systemd service or use the following command at boot:

sudo iptables-restore < /etc/iptables/rules.v4

On Red Hat/CentOS/Fedora-based systems:

The iptables service should automatically restore the rules stored in /etc/sysconfig/iptables when the system reboots, as long as the iptables service is enabled:

sudo systemctl enable iptables

This command ensures that the iptables service is started at boot, and your saved rules are applied.

Switching from Firewalld to IPtables (On CentOS 7+)

In newer versions of CentOS, Fedora, and RHEL (7 and later), the default firewall management tool is firewalld, not IPtables. If you wish to use IPtables instead of firewalld, you need to disable firewalld and enable the IPtables service.

To switch to IPtables, run the following commands:

sudo systemctl stop firewalld
# Stop firewalld

sudo systemctl disable firewalld
# Disable firewalld from starting on boot

sudo systemctl enable iptables
# Enable the IPtables service

sudo systemctl start iptables
# Start the IPtables service immediately

This ensures that IPtables is used instead of firewalld and that your IPtables rules will be applied at boot.

Basic IPtables Architecture: Tables, Chains, and Targets

At its core, IPtables uses a simple architecture consisting of tables, chains, and targets to process network traffic.

Tables: These are containers that define the type of operation to be performed on incoming and outgoing traffic.

There are several built-in tables in IPtables, but the most commonly used are:

filter: This is the default table used for packet filtering. It handles rules related to accepting or blocking packets based on their properties.

nat: This table is used for network address translation (NAT), which modifies the source or destination IP address of packets. It is used primarily for tasks such as masquerading or port forwarding.

mangle: This table is used for specialized packet alteration, such as modifying the Type of Service (TOS) field, marking packets, or other advanced operations.

raw: Used for configuring rules that exempt certain packets from connection tracking.
security: This table is used in conjunction with SELinux to handle rules related to security contexts.

For example, to view the default filter table, the command would be:

sudo iptables -t filter -L

Chains: Each table is divided into chains, which are sets of rules that process packets.

The three main chains in the filter table are:

INPUT: Handles incoming packets destined for the local system.

OUTPUT: Deals with outgoing packets originating from the local system.

FORWARD: Manages packets being routed through the system to other destinations.

When traffic reaches a firewall, it is processed in sequence through these chains based on the type of traffic. For example, if an incoming packet arrives at the system, it is processed by the INPUT chain to determine whether it should be allowed or blocked.

You can add rules to specific chains using the -A (append) option. For example:

sudo iptables -A INPUT -p tcp --dport 22 -j ACCEPT

This rule allows incoming SSH traffic (port 22) by appending the rule to the INPUT chain.

Targets: Each rule in a chain has a corresponding target, which determines the action taken on a packet that matches the rule.

Common targets include:

ACCEPT: Allow the packet to pass through.

DROP: Discard the packet without notifying the sender.

REJECT: Discard the packet and send an error message to the sender.

RETURN: Stops rule processing and returns to the previous chain.

For instance, in the rule above:
sudo iptables -A INPUT -p tcp --dport 22 -j ACCEPT

The target is ACCEPT, meaning the firewall will allow incoming traffic on port 22 (SSH).

Example Configuration – Simple Web Server

NFTables is designed to replace IPtables with a more modern, streamlined interface. Below is the equivalent NFTables configuration for a simple web server setup where only specific ports (SSH, HTTP, HTTPS, FTP) are open, and all other incoming traffic is blocked.

Create a Table for Filtering

First, we need to create a new table where the filtering rules will be stored. We'll use the inet family to handle both IPv4 and IPv6 traffic.

sudo nft add table inet filter

Create Chains for Incoming and Outgoing Traffic

Next, we'll create the necessary chains for handling the incoming (input), outgoing (output), and forwarded (forward) traffic.

sudo nft add chain inet filter input { type filter hook input priority 0 \; }

sudo nft add chain inet filter output { type filter hook output priority 0 \; }

sudo nft add chain inet filter forward { type filter hook forward priority 0 \; }

Add Rules for Allowing Specific Ports
Now, we will define the rules for allowing specific ports.

Allow SSH (Port 22):
```
sudo nft add rule inet filter input tcp dport 22 accept
# Allow SSH
```

Allow HTTP (Port 80):
```
sudo nft add rule inet filter input tcp dport 80 accept
# Allow HTTP
```

Allow HTTPS (Port 443):
```
sudo nft add rule inet filter input tcp dport 443 accept
# Allow HTTPS
```

Allow FTP (Port 21):
```
sudo nft add rule inet filter input tcp dport 21 accept
# Allow FTP
```

Block All Other Incoming Traffic

After allowing the essential ports, we'll block all other incoming traffic:

```
sudo nft add rule inet filter input drop
# Block all other incoming traffic
```

This rule ensures that all traffic not explicitly allowed in the previous rules will be dropped, providing a "default deny" approach.

Verify the Configuration

To check the rules and ensure they were added correctly, you can use the following command:

sudo nft list ruleset

This will display the active ruleset and allow you to confirm that the correct ports are open and others are blocked.

Save the NFTables Rules

To ensure that the rules persist across system reboots, we need to save them to a file. This step is important because unlike IPtables, NFTables does not automatically save its rules upon restart.

sudo nft list ruleset > /etc/nftables.conf

Enable and Start the NFTables Service

Finally, to ensure that NFTables starts automatically at boot and applies the saved configuration, run the following commands:

sudo systemctl enable nftables

sudo systemctl start nftables

This will enable and start the nftables service, ensuring your firewall rules are applied every time the server reboots.

Chapter 5: Working with IPtables Rules

In this chapter, we'll explore the fundamentals of writing and managing IPtables rules to control network traffic on your Linux system. IPtables allows administrators to define rules that either allow or block traffic based on various parameters, such as IP addresses, protocols, or ports. Any Linux server that connects to the outside world will require firewall rules to control these connections. It's essential to configure your firewall rules carefully to prevent potential risks and ensure your server operates securely and efficiently.

Commonly Used Ports On Linux Servers

Linux servers often utilize a wide range of ports to facilitate various network services and applications. Each port is associated with a specific protocol or service, and understanding these ports is crucial for managing server security and functionality. Below is a list of commonly used ports on Linux servers, many of which can be controlled or restricted using Iptables or other firewall tools to allow or block traffic based on your server's needs.

20, 21 – FTP (File Transfer Protocol)
Port 21 is used for FTP commands.

Port 20 is used for FTP data transfer.

22 – SSH (Secure Shell)
Used for remote login and secure file transfers (e.g., scp, sftp).

25 – SMTP (Simple Mail Transfer Protocol)
Used for sending emails.

53 – DNS (Domain Name System)
Used for domain name resolution.

67, 68 – DHCP (Dynamic Host Configuration Protocol)
Used for dynamically assigning IP addresses to devices on a network.

80 – HTTP (HyperText Transfer Protocol)
Used for serving web pages over an unsecured connection.

110 – POP3 (Post Office Protocol)
Used for retrieving emails from a remote server.

123 – NTP (Network Time Protocol)
Used for clock synchronization between computer systems.

143 – IMAP (Internet Message Access Protocol)
Used for accessing emails on a remote server.

443 – HTTPS (HyperText Transfer Protocol Secure)
Used for serving web pages over a secure, encrypted connection (SSL/TLS).

465 – SMTPS (SMTP Secure)
Used for sending emails securely over SSL/TLS.

993 – IMAPS (IMAP Secure)
Secure version of IMAP, encrypted with SSL/TLS.

995 – POP3S (POP3 Secure)
Secure version of POP3, encrypted with SSL/TLS.

3306 – MySQL/MariaDB
Used for database connections to MySQL or MariaDB databases.

5432 – PostgreSQL
Used for database connections to PostgreSQL databases.

6379 – Redis
Used for in-memory database and caching service.

8080 – Alternative HTTP
Often used as an alternative port for HTTP web traffic.

8443 – Alternative HTTPS
Often used as an alternative port for HTTPS web traffic (secure).

10000 – Webmin
Used for web-based administration of Unix/Linux systems.

3000, 5000 – Custom Application Ports
Commonly used for custom web applications and development servers.

Additional Common Ports:

5900 – VNC (Virtual Network Computing) (used for remote desktop access).
25, 587 – SMTP (often 587 is used for secure email submission with STARTTLS).

993, 995 – IMAP/POP3 Secure (used for secure email retrieval).

Ports for Video and Audio Streaming

1935 – RTMP (Real-Time Messaging Protocol)

RTMP is a common protocol used for streaming audio, video, and data over the Internet. It is widely used for live streaming and is supported by platforms like YouTube, Twitch, and Facebook Live.

554 – RTSP (Real-Time Streaming Protocol)
RTSP is used for establishing and controlling media sessions between endpoints. It's a control protocol designed for real-time media streaming.

8554 – RTSP Alternative
Some RTSP implementations use port 8554 instead of 554 to avoid conflicts with other services.

8000, 8001 – Shoutcast/Icecast
These ports are often used for audio streaming by Shoutcast and Icecast servers. Icecast is commonly used for Internet radio.

1755 – MMS (Microsoft Media Server Protocol)
MMS is an older streaming protocol used primarily for streaming audio and video from Windows Media servers.

5004, 5005 – RTP (Real-Time Transport Protocol)
RTP is used for delivering audio and video over IP networks. It's often used in conjunction with RTSP for streaming and VoIP (Voice over IP) services.

8800 – HTTP Live Streaming (HLS)
HLS is a media streaming protocol used to deliver live and on-demand content over HTTP. Although it primarily uses HTTP ports (80 and 443), some custom implementations may use port 8800 or similar.

8080 – Alternative HTTP Streaming
Some services use port 8080 for HTTP-based streaming as an alternative to the standard port 80.

10000 – WebRTC (Web Real-Time Communication)

WebRTC allows for audio, video, and data sharing directly between browsers without needing plugins. It uses a range of dynamic ports, often starting at port 10000 (UDP) for interactive media sessions.

6970-6999 – QuickTime Streaming Server (QTSS)
QuickTime uses these ports for audio and video streaming.

3478-3481 – STUN/TURN (Session Traversal Utilities for NAT)
STUN and TURN are protocols used to traverse NAT (Network Address Translation) and allow peer-to-peer communication, often used in video conferencing and VoIP services.

Other Ports Relevant to Media Streaming

80, 443 – HTTP/HTTPS
Streaming services that use HTTP-based protocols (like HLS or DASH) for streaming often use the standard HTTP (80) or HTTPS (443) ports.

53 – DNS (Domain Name System)
Though not specific to streaming, DNS is essential for resolving domain names to IP addresses before accessing streaming services.

19302-19309 – Google STUN Servers (WebRTC)
These ports are used for WebRTC peer-to-peer connections, including audio and video calls.

10000-20000 (UDP) – VoIP and Streaming Ports
For VoIP and real-time video/audio streaming, UDP ports within this range are often used. Many streaming protocols dynamically assign UDP ports within this range.

Printer Ports:

515 – LPD/LPR (Line Printer Daemon)

A legacy protocol used for network printing. Commonly used on Unix/Linux systems to queue and send print jobs to networked printers.

631 – IPP (Internet Printing Protocol)
IPP is the default protocol used by modern printers and CUPS (Common Unix Printing System). It allows for printing, managing jobs, and querying printer status over a network.

9100 – RAW Port for Printing (JetDirect/RAW)
Used by many network printers (especially HP printers) for direct (RAW) printing. Often called the JetDirect protocol.

137-139, 445 – SMB/CIFS (Samba Printing)
Used for Windows file and print sharing over a network. If your Linux system is set up with Samba to allow printing via SMB, it will use these ports for communication.

Ports for Ham Radio Servers

EchoLink (VoIP for ham radio)
UDP 5198-5199: Used for voice communication.
TCP 5200: Used for connection to the EchoLink directory.

AllStarLink (Radio-over-IP for linking repeaters)
UDP 4569: AllStarLink protocol for VoIP-based communication.

D-STAR (Digital Smart Technologies for Amateur Radio)
UDP 20000-20010: Used for D-STAR repeater links and communication.

DMR (Digital Mobile Radio)
UDP 62031: Used for DMR gateways and communication between repeaters and hotspots.

Ports for Minecraft Servers

Java Edition (default port):
TCP 25565: The default port for Minecraft Java Edition. If you're hosting a Java server, this is the port that needs to be open.

Bedrock Edition (default port):
UDP 19132: The default port for Minecraft Bedrock Edition, used for both internal and external connections.

Special/Reserved Ports:

1–1023 – System Ports (privileged ports, used by well-known services).

1024–49151 – User Ports (registered for user services and applications).

49152–65535 – Dynamic/Private Ports (typically used for client-side ephemeral ports during communication).

Writing Basic IPtables Rules

Writing IPtables rules is straightforward once you understand its syntax. Rules follow a format where you specify the chain (e.g., INPUT, OUTPUT, FORWARD), the protocol (e.g., TCP, UDP), and the action (e.g., ACCEPT, DROP).

For example, to allow incoming HTTP traffic on port 80, you would use:

```
sudo iptables -A INPUT -p tcp --dport 80 -j ACCEPT
```

This rule adds (-A) a new entry to the INPUT chain that allows (-j ACCEPT) TCP traffic targeting port 80 (HTTP).

Allowing or Blocking Specific IP Addresses, Protocols, or Ports

You can also write rules to allow or block specific IP addresses or ranges.

For example, to block incoming traffic from a particular IP address (e.g., 192.168.1.100), the rule would be:

sudo iptables -A INPUT -s 192.168.1.100 -j DROP

To block all incoming traffic from an IP range:

sudo iptables -A INPUT -s 192.168.1.0/24 -j DROP

The asterisk (*) represents a range of IP addresses, and in this case, the range covers all IPs from **192.168.1.0 to 192.168.1.255**.

Similarly, you can block traffic on a specific protocol or port. For instance, to block all incoming FTP traffic (port 21), use:

```
sudo iptables -A INPUT -p tcp --dport 21 -j DROP
```

This flexibility makes IPtables a powerful tool for tailoring your firewall to suit specific security needs.

Manipulating and Managing IPtables Rules

IPtables allows administrators to add, remove, or list rules as needed. To add a rule, use the -A (append) option, while removing a rule can be done using the -D (delete) option.

For example, to remove the rule allowing HTTP traffic, use:

```
sudo iptables -D INPUT -p tcp --dport 80 -j ACCEPT
```

To list all current rules, you can use:

```
sudo iptables -L
```

This command will display the active IPtables rules, allowing you to review and adjust as necessary.

Chapter 6: IPtables for Network Address Translation (NAT)

Source and destination NAT (SNAT/DNAT) explained

Network Address Translation (NAT) is a technique used to modify the source or destination IP address of packets as they pass through a router or firewall. IPtables provides a powerful way to configure NAT on Linux systems, allowing administrators to control how network traffic is routed between internal and external networks. In this chapter, we will cover the basic concepts of Source NAT (SNAT) and Destination NAT (DNAT), as well as how to configure port forwarding and masquerading for efficient network routing.

Source NAT (SNAT)

Source NAT is used to modify the source IP address of outgoing packets. This is typically used when a device on a private internal network needs to communicate with external servers. SNAT hides the internal IP address and replaces it with the public IP address of the router or firewall. This is particularly useful when multiple devices on a local network share a single public IP address.

Example: A machine with an internal IP address of 192.168.1.2 wants to access the internet. With SNAT, the source address of packets from 192.168.1.2 will be changed to the public IP of the firewall.

To implement SNAT with IPtables, use the following command:

sudo iptables -t nat -A POSTROUTING -s 192.168.1.0/24 -o eth0 -j SNAT --to-source 203.0.113.10

Explanation

-t nat: Specifies the NAT table.

-A POSTROUTING: Appends the rule to the POSTROUTING chain, which is used for outgoing packets.

-s 192.168.1.0/24: Specifies the source network to be translated.

-o eth0: Specifies the outgoing interface (e.g., eth0 for the external network).

-j SNAT: Performs source NAT.

--to-source 203.0.113.10: Replaces the source IP with the public IP address of the router (203.0.113.10).

Destination NAT (DNAT)

Destination NAT is used to modify the destination IP address of incoming packets. DNAT is commonly used for port forwarding, where external traffic directed to a specific port on a public IP address is forwarded to an internal server. This is useful for scenarios where services like web servers, FTP servers, or game servers are running behind a firewall.

Example: If you want to forward HTTP traffic (port 80) from the public IP address 203.0.113.10 to an internal web server with the IP address 192.168.1.5, you can use DNAT.

To implement DNAT with IPtables, use the following command:

sudo iptables -t nat -A PREROUTING -p tcp --dport 80 -j DNAT --to-destination 192.168.1.5

Explanation

-t nat: Specifies the NAT table.

-A PREROUTING: Appends the rule to the PREROUTING chain, which is used for incoming packets.

-p tcp: Specifies the protocol (TCP in this case).

--dport 80: Specifies the destination port (port 80 for HTTP).

-j DNAT: Performs destination NAT.

--to-destination 192.168.1.5: Redirects the traffic to the internal IP address 192.168.1.5.

Port Forwarding and Masquerading

Port Forwarding

Port forwarding allows traffic from an external network (usually the internet) to reach specific services hosted on an internal network. Port forwarding is typically implemented using DNAT to forward packets to the correct internal IP address based on the port.

Real Example of Usage:

Imagine you are hosting a web server on your home network with the internal IP address 192.168.1.10, but your internet service provider only assigns you a single public IP address. To make your web server accessible to users on the internet, you can set up port forwarding on your Linux server. You would configure IPtables to forward all incoming traffic on port 80 (HTTP) to the internal IP address 192.168.1.10:80. When someone visits your public IP address (e.g., 203.0.113.1), IPtables forwards their request to your internal web server, allowing external users to access your website without exposing the rest of your network.

Another example, to forward SSH traffic (port 22) to an internal server with the IP 192.168.1.10:

```
sudo iptables -t nat -A PREROUTING -p tcp --dport 22
-j DNAT --to-destination 192.168.1.10:22
```

This rule forwards incoming TCP traffic on port 22 to the internal server at 192.168.1.10 on the same port.

Masquerading

Masquerading is a form of SNAT where the source IP of outgoing packets is dynamically replaced with the IP address of the outgoing interface (usually the public IP of the firewall). This is particularly useful in home or small office networks where multiple internal devices share a single public IP address.

Real Example of Usage:

Imagine you have a small office network with several computers (e.g., 192.168.1.10, 192.168.1.11, 192.168.1.12) that need to access the internet. Your internet service provider assigns you only one public IP address (e.g., 203.0.113.1). To enable all the internal devices to access the internet while sharing this single public IP, you would configure IP masquerading on your Linux server, which acts as a firewall and router for your network.

Here's how you can set up masquerading using IPtables on the Linux server:

Enable IP Forwarding

First, you need to enable IP forwarding on the Linux server

so it can route packets between the internal network and the internet:

```
echo 1 > /proc/sys/net/ipv4/ip_forward
```

Alternatively, you can make this change permanent by editing /etc/sysctl.conf and adding:

```
net.ipv4.ip_forward = 1
```

Configure IP Masquerading with IPtables

Next, you'll configure IPtables to masquerade traffic coming from your internal network (e.g., 192.168.1.0/24) and going out through the public interface (e.g., eth0):

```
iptables -t nat -A POSTROUTING -o eth0 -s 192.168.1.0/24 -j MASQUERADE
```

In this command:

-t nat: Specifies the **NAT** table.

-A POSTROUTING: Adds a rule to the POSTROUTING chain, which alters packets after the routing decision has been made.

-o eth0: Specifies the outgoing interface, usually the public-facing one.

-s 192.168.1.0/24: Defines the source network (your internal network).

-j MASQUERADE: Tells IPtables to masquerade the packets, dynamically replacing the source IP address with the public IP of the eth0 interface.

Save the IPtables Rules:

To ensure the rules persist after a reboot, save the IPtables configuration:

```
iptables-save > /etc/iptables/rules.v4
```

How It Works:

When an internal device (e.g., 192.168.1.10) sends a request to access a website, the Linux server modifies the source IP of the outgoing packets to its public IP (e.g., 203.0.113.1).

The website server responds to the public IP address (203.0.113.1), and when the Linux server receives the response, it rewrites the destination IP back to the internal IP (192.168.1.10) and forwards it to the correct device.

This allows all internal devices to share a single public IP while keeping the internal network isolated and secure.

Using NAT for Routing Traffic Between Internal and External Networks

NAT can be used to route traffic between an internal network and an external network (such as the internet). This is typically done when a private network needs access to the internet but does not have its own public IP addresses.

For example, you can use SNAT and DNAT to allow internal clients to access the internet and allow external access to a specific internal service.

Allowing Internal Clients to Access the Internet

If you want internal clients on a private network (192.168.1.0/24) to access the internet via a router with a public IP, you can use SNAT:

```
sudo iptables -t nat -A POSTROUTING -s
192.168.1.0/24 -o eth0 -j MASQUERADE
```

This rule ensures that packets originating from the 192.168.1.0/24 network have their source address changed to the public IP address of eth0, allowing them to reach external destinations.

Allowing External Access to an Internal Service

To allow external access to a service hosted on an internal machine (e.g., a web server with IP 192.168.1.10), you can

use DNAT:

```
sudo iptables -t nat -A PREROUTING -p tcp --dport 80
-j DNAT --to-destination 192.168.1.10:80
```

This rule forwards external HTTP traffic (port 80) to the internal web server at 192.168.1.10.

Chapter 7: Advanced IPtables Features

Creating Custom Chains

In this chapter, we will delve deeper into the advanced features of IPtables, a powerful tool used in Linux for managing network traffic through the creation of firewall rules. Beyond basic filtering, IPtables offers a wide range of capabilities that can help secure and manage your network more effectively. We will cover the following advanced features: custom chains, rate limiting and connection tracking, and logging and debugging firewall rules.

Creating Custom Chains

By default, IPtables uses three built-in chains for managing traffic: INPUT, OUTPUT, and FORWARD. However, there are situations where you may need to create your own chains to better organize and control your firewall rules.

Custom Chains allow you to create specialized traffic flows and apply more granular rules. Instead of cluttering the default chains with many rules, you can create custom chains that are referenced in your rulesets.

Creating custom chains is done using the iptables -N command, followed by the name of your new chain. Once created, you can add rules to your custom chain just as you would with the built-in ones.

Custom chains can be used to streamline complex configurations and provide more flexibility in traffic control. You can also direct traffic from one chain to another for greater modularity in your firewall setup.

Create a custom chain called "MYCHAIN":
sudo iptables -N MYCHAIN

Add rules to the custom chain:
sudo iptables -A MYCHAIN -p tcp --dport 80 -j ACCEPT
sudo iptables -A MYCHAIN -p tcp --dport 443 -j ACCEPT

Link the custom chain to the INPUT chain:
sudo iptables -A INPUT -j MYCHAIN

This example shows how a custom chain (MYCHAIN) is created and linked to the INPUT chain, allowing specific rules for HTTP and HTTPS traffic.

Rate Limiting, Connection Tracking, Logging/Debug

IPtables can be used to control the rate of incoming connections or requests to protect against DDoS (Distributed Denial of Service) attacks or to ensure fair use of resources. This can be achieved through rate limiting and connection tracking.

Rate Limiting allows you to set a limit on the number of connections or packets from a single IP address within a specified time frame. This can prevent abusive or malicious users from overwhelming the server or network with excessive traffic.

The limit module in IPtables allows you to define a rate limit. For example, you can restrict new connections to a maximum of 3 per second.

This is done using the -m limit option in conjunction with the --limit parameter.

Limit new incoming connections to 3 per second per IP address:

```
sudo iptables -A INPUT -p tcp --dport 80 -m limit --limit 3/second -j ACCEPT
```

Connection Tracking keeps track of the state of network connections (e.g., new, established, or related) and allows for more advanced filtering based on the connection state. The state module in IPtables enables connection tracking, allowing you to accept or block packets based on whether they are part of an existing connection or a new connection.

This is useful for ensuring that only legitimate traffic is allowed through, such as permitting only established connections on the INPUT chain.

Allow traffic for established connections:

```
sudo iptables -A INPUT -m state --state ESTABLISHED,RELATED -j ACCEPT
```

Logging and Debugging Firewall Rules

When troubleshooting firewall rules, it's essential to be able to log network activity and diagnose issues effectively. IPtables provides built-in logging features to capture packet information and help you debug rules.

Logging network activity is a crucial step in monitoring and debugging firewall behavior. The LOG target in IPtables logs packets that match a rule but doesn't affect the flow of traffic (i.e., the packet continues to be processed by subsequent rules).

Logs are typically written to /var/log/messages or /var/log/syslog, depending on the system configuration.

Log all incoming traffic on port 22 (SSH):

sudo iptables -A INPUT -p tcp --dport 22 -j LOG --log-prefix "SSH Attempt:"

This rule will log all SSH attempts with the prefix SSH Attempt:, making it easy to identify in the log file.

Logging Network Activity on Debian-based Systems with systemd Journal

Logging network activity with IPtables on Debian-based systems (like Ubuntu) is often configured to write logs to the systemd journal instead of traditional log files. This means that logs may not appear in /var/log/syslog or /var/log/messages by default, but instead can be accessed using the journalctl command.

Using the LOG Target in IPtables

As with traditional logging, you can still use the LOG target in IPtables to log network traffic, but the logs will go to the systemd journal by default.

Here's an example rule that logs all incoming SSH traffic (port 22) with a specific log prefix:

sudo iptables -A INPUT -p tcp --dport 22 -j LOG --log-prefix "SSH Attempt:"

--log-prefix "SSH Attempt: ": This option adds a label to each log entry, making it easier to identify.

-j LOG: This specifies the log target, meaning packets matching this rule will be logged.

Viewing Logs in the Journal

Since Debian-based systems using systemd write logs to the journal by default, you can view the logs using the journalctl command. To see the logs for the rule above, you would run:

sudo journalctl -t iptables

-t iptables: This option filters logs by the specific identifier iptables, which should capture entries created by IPtables logging.

Alternatively, to filter logs for SSH traffic specifically, you can use grep to look for your log prefix:

sudo journalctl | grep "SSH Attempt:"

This will display entries in the journal that include the "SSH Attempt:" prefix, allowing you to see all SSH-related log events.

Persistent Logging

In some cases, you might want to make sure the logs persist in files (like /var/log/iptables.log) for easier analysis or archival purposes.

You can do this by configuring rsyslog or systemd-journald to forward the logs to specific log files. For example, to forward IPtables logs to a dedicated file:

Edit /etc/rsyslog.d/iptables.conf (or create it if it doesn't exist).

Add a rule to forward logs related to IPtables:

```
:msg, contains, "SSH Attempt:" /var/log/iptables.log
```

Restart the rsyslog service:

```
sudo systemctl restart rsyslog
```

Now, any log entries that match the specified message (e.g., "SSH Attempt:") will be saved in /var/log/iptables.log, allowing you to easily access and monitor the logs.

Debugging IPtables rules can sometimes be challenging, especially if you have complex rule sets. Fortunately, IPtables offers a few strategies to help debug:

List rules with verbose output: Using iptables -L -v will display rule counts, packet statistics, and additional information.

Flush and Reset Rules: If you suspect that the current rule set is too complex or misconfigured, you can flush the rules using iptables -F and start fresh.
Example

Display IPtables rules with verbose output:
sudo iptables -L -v

This command will provide detailed information about the current IPtables rule set, including packet counts and byte statistics.

Part 3: Transitioning to NFTables

Chapter 8: Why NFTables?

Introduction to NFTables and its advantages over IPtables

As the successor to IPtables, NFTables brings a host of improvements that address the shortcomings of IPtables while maintaining the functionality and flexibility required for modern network traffic filtering. In this chapter, we will explore why NFTables is the recommended firewall solution for current Linux systems, its key advantages over IPtables, and the fundamental differences between the two. Finally, we'll discuss how to transition from IPtables to NFTables seamlessly.

NFTables was introduced as part of the Linux kernel in version 3.13 to replace the older IPtables framework. While IPtables served its purpose for many years, NFTables provides a more streamlined, efficient, and powerful approach to network filtering. It is designed to be more flexible, support modern hardware architectures, and offer better performance with less complexity.

Key advantages of NFTables over IPtables include:

Unified Framework: Unlike IPtables, which required separate modules for IPv4, IPv6, ARP, and more, NFTables unifies all these protocols under a single framework. This simplifies rule management and reduces the need for multiple tools.

Improved Performance: NFTables introduces a more efficient data structure known as the "rule set", which helps to improve performance, especially in complex rule sets. It eliminates the need for repeated traversal of the rules for each packet, making the filtering process faster.

Easier Syntax: The syntax for defining rules in NFTables is more user-friendly than IPtables, making it easier for administrators to write and manage complex rules. The rule definitions are more concise and follow a consistent format.

Support for Newer Technologies: NFTables supports new technologies such as eBPF (Extended Berkeley Packet Filter), which enhances the capability to run custom programs at various points in the networking stack. This makes it more flexible and extensible for modern applications.

Atomic Rule Updates: NFTables allows atomic rule updates, meaning that updates to firewall rules can be done without causing downtime. In contrast, IPtables often required flushing and reloading the entire rule set, leading to brief periods of traffic disruption.

Stateful Filtering and NAT (Network Address Translation): NFTables brings native support for both stateful packet inspection and NAT in a single unified framework. In IPtables, these features were handled by separate modules, leading to more complex configurations.

Key Differences Between IPtables and NFTables

While both IPtables and NFTables aim to perform the same fundamental task—network packet filtering—they differ in several important ways.

Below are the key differences that define the shift from IPtables to NFTables:

Architecture

IPtables: IPtables uses a set of separate chains for IPv4, IPv6, ARP, and other protocols. Each protocol has its own set of rules, making it more complex to manage multiple protocol types.

NFTables: NFTables consolidates all these protocols into one unified framework, using tables, chains, and sets that can support different types of rules and conditions.

Rule Set Management

IPtables: Each chain in IPtables operates independently. To optimize filtering, complex rules could require manually managing the order and structure of the chains.

NFTables: NFTables uses a more flexible rule set approach. The rule set can be managed in a single place, reducing the need for multiple tools and providing better control over the filtering process.

Performance

IPtables: IPtables performance can degrade as the number of rules increases, particularly when dealing with large, complex rule sets, as it needs to evaluate each rule sequentially.

NFTables: NFTables improves on this by using an optimized netlink-based **architecture** that handles large rule sets more efficiently, leading to better overall performance.

Syntax and Configuration

IPtables: The IPtables command syntax is more verbose and requires administrators to manually specify the rule parameters for each protocol.

NFTables: NFTables uses a more straightforward and consistent syntax that reduces complexity in rule definitions.

For example, with NFTables, you can define rules for multiple protocols in one place, reducing duplication.

Stateful and Stateless Processing

IPtables: IPtables supports stateful packet inspection, but it does so using a more complicated setup that requires loading various modules like state and conntrack.

NFTables: In NFTables, stateful filtering is built into the rule structure, making it easier to configure and manage.

NAT

IPtables: NAT functionality is separate in IPtables and managed through its NAT table. Complex NAT setups can be difficult to manage with IPtables.

NFTables: In NFTables, NAT is integrated directly into the firewall framework, simplifying configuration and management.

Transitioning from IPtables to NFTables

The transition from IPtables to NFTables may seem daunting, but it is necessary to take advantage of the performance improvements and modern features offered by NFTables.

Fortunately, transitioning is made easier through the following steps:

Compatibility

NFTables provides compatibility with existing IPtables rules via the iptables-translate tool. This tool helps convert existing IPtables rules into NFTables syntax, making the migration smoother.

Coexistence

You can run IPtables and NFTables concurrently during the migration process. This allows you to test NFTables while maintaining your current IPtables setup. However, it's important to ensure that there are no conflicts between the two systems during the transition.

Converting Rules

Use the iptables-translate command to convert existing IPtables rule sets to NFTables format:

```
sudo   iptables-translate   -f   /etc/iptables/rules.v4   >
/etc/nftables.conf
```

After converting the rules, you can load them into NFTables using the nft command.

Understanding the New Syntax

Familiarize yourself with the new NFTables syntax, which is more streamlined than IPtables. You can define tables, chains, and rules using the nft command, and more complex configurations can be handled via scripts.

Example

```
sudo nft add table inet filter

sudo nft add chain inet filter input { type filter hook input priority 0 \; }

sudo nft add rule inet filter input ip daddr 192.168.1.1 accept
```

Testing and Validation

Before fully deprecating IPtables, thoroughly test your NFTables configuration in a staging environment to ensure everything works as expected. Use tools like nft list ruleset to review the active rules and validate traffic flow.

Disabling IPtables

Once you're confident that your NFTables rules are working correctly, you can disable IPtables to ensure that NFTables is the only active firewall system on the server.

sudo systemctl stop iptables

sudo systemctl disable iptables

Final Cleanup

After the transition is complete, remove any legacy IPtables rules or configurations that are no longer needed to maintain a clean, manageable firewall setup.

Chapter 9: Getting Started with NFTables

History and Role of NFTables in Linux Systems

NFTables was introduced in Linux kernel version 3.13 as a replacement for the older IPtables framework, aiming to provide a more modern, efficient, and flexible packet filtering system. Its primary role in Linux systems is to control network traffic through rules and policies, ensuring secure and optimized data flow. NFTables combines the functionality of several previous frameworks, including IPtables, IP6tables, ARP tables, and ebtables, into a single unified framework, simplifying management. It offers improvements such as a more efficient rule processing engine, better syntax, and enhanced support for both IPv4 and IPv6. The modular architecture of NFTables also allows for easier extension and future feature additions, making it a more scalable solution for network traffic filtering and security. As Linux systems increasingly rely on NFTables, it plays a pivotal role in securing servers, workstations, and networked devices, supporting everything from simple firewall configurations to advanced traffic management and load balancing.

Installing NFTables

NFTables is included by default in most modern Linux distributions with the nft utility available in the system's package manager. If you're using an older system or a distribution that doesn't have NFTables installed, you can install it manually.

Debian/Ubuntu:

To install NFTables on Debian-based systems (e.g., Ubuntu), use the following commands:

sudo apt update

sudo apt install nftables

CentOS/RHEL:

On Red Hat-based distributions (e.g., CentOS, RHEL), NFTables is included by default in recent versions. If it's not installed, you can install it with:

```
sudo yum install nftables
```

Arch Linux:

On Arch Linux and its derivatives, you can install NFTables with:

```
sudo pacman -S nftables
```

After installation, you can check the version and ensure it's installed correctly by running:

```
nft --version
```

Configuring NFTables Rules

NFTables configuration is based on a few basic concepts:

Tables, Chains, and Rules. Each of these elements helps you define how network traffic is filtered and processed.

Basic Components

Table: A table is a container for chains. It defines the type of filtering or processing to be done.

Chain: Chains define the order and conditions under which rules are applied. Chains can be attached to specific hooks in the packet processing flow.

Rule: A rule specifies a condition for processing a packet. It can either accept, drop, or log the packet.

In the example below, we will configure NFTables for basic packet filtering. We'll create a table, add chains, and define rules for controlling traffic.

Create a Table

First, create a table for filtering network traffic. We'll use the inet family because it supports both IPv4 and IPv6 traffic.

```
sudo nft add table inet filter
```

This creates a new table called filter in the inet family.

Create Chains

Next, we'll create three chains for managing different types of traffic:

input: For incoming traffic to the local machine.

output: For outgoing traffic from the machine.

forward: For traffic being routed through the machine.

```
sudo nft add chain inet filter input { type filter hook
input priority 0 \; }
```

```
sudo nft add chain inet filter output { type filter hook
output priority 0 \; }
```

```
sudo nft add chain inet filter forward { type filter hook
forward priority 0 \; }
```

These chains are attached to the input, output, and forward packet hooks, meaning they will process packets at the appropriate stage in the packet processing flow.

Define Rules

Now, we define rules that specify how traffic should be handled based on conditions.

Allow SSH (Port 22)

This rule allows incoming SSH traffic (port 22) on the input chain:

```
sudo nft add rule inet filter input tcp dport 22 accept
```

This rule checks if the incoming packet is a TCP packet with a destination port of 22 (SSH), and if it matches, it will accept the packet.

Allow HTTP (Port 80)

This rule allows HTTP traffic (port 80) on the input chain:

```
sudo nft add rule inet filter input tcp dport 80 accept
```

This rule allows incoming packets with destination port 80, which is commonly used for HTTP traffic.

Allow HTTPS (Port 443)

This rule allows HTTPS traffic (port 443) on the input chain:

sudo nft add rule inet filter input tcp dport 443 accept

This rule permits packets with destination port 443, used for secure HTTPS connections.

Block All Other Incoming Traffic

This rule blocks all other incoming traffic by default:

sudo nft add rule inet filter input drop

Any packet that does not match a previous rule will be dropped. This ensures that only specific traffic (SSH, HTTP, HTTPS) is allowed, and all other traffic is denied.

Verify the Configuration

To verify the rules and check the active ruleset, you can use the following command:

sudo nft list ruleset

This will display the current configuration of tables, chains, and rules.

Saving NFTables Rules

Once you've configured your firewall rules with NFTables, you'll need to save them to ensure they persist after a reboot. NFTables does not save rules automatically by default.

Saving Rules
To save the active rules to a file, use the nft utility.

For example:

sudo nft list ruleset > /etc/nftables.conf

This command writes the current ruleset to the file /etc/nftables.conf.

Restoring NFTables Rules

If you need to restore your saved rules after a reboot or from a backup, you can use the nft command to load the rules from the saved file.

Restoring Rules

To restore the saved ruleset, run:

sudo nft -f /etc/nftables.conf

This will load the rules from the specified file and apply them to your active firewall.

Verify the Restored Rules:

After restoring, it's a good idea to verify that the rules have been applied correctly by listing the active ruleset:

sudo nft list ruleset

Enabling NFTables to Start at Boot

To ensure NFTables starts automatically on boot, enable the systemd service:

```
sudo systemctl enable nftables
sudo systemctl start nftables
```

This ensures that your firewall rules are loaded every time the system starts.

Basic NFTables Architecture: Tables, Chains, and Sets

NFTables' architecture revolves around **tables**, **chains**, and **sets**. Let's break down these components.

Tables: A table contains one or more chains and is used to define how packets should be processed (filtering, NAT, etc.). The type of table can define what kind of processing should occur.

There are several types of tables:

filter: Used for packet filtering (default).

nat: Used for NAT (Network Address Translation).

mangle: Used for packet mangling (modifying packets).

route: Used for routing decisions.

Chains: Chains are containers for rules. Chains define the packet flow path in the firewall, specifying hooks at certain points in the network stack. The most common chains are:

input: Handles incoming traffic.

output: Handles outgoing traffic.

forward: Handles traffic that is routed through the system.

Each chain can be tied to specific actions (accept, drop, log, etc.), and they are processed in the order they are defined.

Sets: A set in NFTables is a collection of elements (e.g., IP addresses, ports) that can be used in rules. Sets improve performance by allowing multiple values to be handled as a single entity. For example, you can define a set of allowed IP addresses and use it in your rules.

Example of defining a set:

sudo nft add set inet filter allowed_ips { type ipv4_addr\; }

```
sudo nft add element inet filter allowed_ips { 192.168.1.10,
192.168.1.20 }
```

You can now refer to this set in rules:

```
sudo nft add rule inet filter input ip saddr @allowed_ips accept
```

Example Configuration – Simple Web Server

Let's summarize an example configuration for a simple web
server:

Create a table for filtering:

```
sudo nft add table inet filter
```

Create chains:

```
sudo nft add chain inet filter input { type filter hook
input priority 0 \; }
```

```
sudo nft add chain inet filter output { type filter hook
output priority 0 \; }
```

```
sudo nft add chain inet filter forward { type filter hook
forward priority 0 \; }
```

Add rules to allow HTTP and HTTPS traffic:

sudo nft add rule inet filter input tcp dport { 80, 443 } accept

Drop other incoming traffic:

sudo nft add rule inet filter input drop

Save the rules:

sudo nft list ruleset > /etc/nftables.conf

Enable NFTables on boot:

sudo systemctl enable nftables

sudo systemctl start nftables

This basic example configures a simple firewall that allows web traffic on ports 80 and 443, drops other incoming traffic, and saves the rules for future use.

Chapter 10: Complex Filtering with NFTables

Combining IPv4 and IPv6 rules

NFTables provides a unified framework for both IPv4 and IPv6, enabling network administrators to handle both types of traffic in a seamless and efficient way. Unlike the older IPtables framework, which required separate rules for IPv4 (using iptables) and IPv6 (using ip6tables), NFTables allows administrators to configure both types of traffic within a single ruleset. This reduces complexity and allows for more comprehensive security policies across both IPv4 and IPv6 networks.

In this chapter, we will explore how to combine IPv4 and IPv6 rules in NFTables, providing examples of how to configure these rules within a single, unified system.

Unified Rule Sets for IPv4 and IPv6

NFTables uses the inet family, which supports both IPv4 and IPv6 traffic simultaneously. This enables the creation of rules that can apply to both address families with a single command.

For example, the following command creates a table that can filter both IPv4 and IPv6 traffic:

```
sudo nft add table inet filter
```

This command defines a filter table in the inet family, where rules for both IPv4 and IPv6 can be applied together.

Defining Chains for IPv4 and IPv6

Within the inet family, you can define chains (e.g., input, output, forward) that handle both types of traffic in the same way.

Let's create an input chain that will apply to both IPv4 and IPv6 traffic:

```
sudo nft add chain inet filter input { type filter hook input priority 0 \; }
```

This chain will process packets from both IPv4 and IPv6 sources, applying the rules defined for it.

Combined Rules for Both IPv4 and IPv6

Once the table and chains are defined, you can create rules that will apply to both IPv4 and IPv6 traffic.

For instance, if you want to allow incoming SSH connections (port 22) for both IPv4 and IPv6, you can use the following command:

```
sudo nft add rule inet filter input tcp dport 22 accept
```

This rule will apply to both IPv4 and IPv6 packets that are destined for port 22 (SSH), and it will accept them, allowing the connection.

Filtering Specific IPv4 or IPv6 Traffic

While NFTables allows you to combine IPv4 and IPv6 rules, there may be cases where you need to filter traffic from one address family but not the other.

For example, to allow IPv4 HTTP traffic on port 80 but block IPv6 HTTP traffic, you can specify the address family in the rule:

Allow HTTP (Port 80) for IPv4 only:

sudo nft add rule ip filter input tcp dport 80 accept

Block HTTP (Port 80) for IPv6 only:

sudo nft add rule ip6 filter input tcp dport 80 drop

In the examples above:

The ip family is used to filter only IPv4 traffic.

The ip6 family is used to filter only IPv6 traffic.

This allows fine-grained control, ensuring that specific address families are handled differently when necessary.

Combining Rules for More Complex Filtering

NFTables also allows for more advanced filtering combinations. For instance, you might want to allow both SSH (Port 22) and HTTP (Port 80) for IPv4 traffic but only allow HTTPS (Port 443) for IPv6.

This would be achieved with the following rules:

Allow SSH and HTTP for IPv4:

sudo nft add rule ip filter input tcp dport {22, 80} accept

Allow HTTPS for IPv6 only:

sudo nft add rule ip6 filter input tcp dport 443 accept

Here:

The {22, 80} syntax allows for multiple ports to be accepted at once for IPv4 traffic.

The second rule explicitly applies only to IPv6 traffic, allowing HTTPS (Port 443).

Default Drop Policy for Both IPv4 and IPv6

For security purposes, it's often recommended to set a default drop policy to block any other traffic that doesn't match your defined rules.

You can apply this to both IPv4 and IPv6 in a unified manner:

sudo nft add rule inet filter input drop

This rule ensures that any packet that doesn't match an accept rule (for either IPv4 or IPv6) is dropped. It's a great way to implement a "default deny" approach that minimizes the attack surface by blocking unwanted traffic.

Using Named Sets for Efficient Rule Management

One of the powerful features of NFTables is the ability to use named sets. Sets in NFTables are collections of items (such as IP addresses, ports, or protocols) that you can reference in your rules. Named sets allow you to group multiple items together and reference them with a single name, streamlining rule management and making the configuration more efficient and scalable. This is particularly useful when you need to apply the same rule to multiple items, as it reduces redundancy and enhances readability.

What Are Named Sets?

A named set is a collection of elements (e.g., IP addresses, IP ranges, ports, etc.) that are assigned a specific name. This name can then be used in the rules, allowing for more organized and dynamic rule management. Named sets are dynamic, meaning you can add or remove elements from the set without modifying the rules that reference the set. This is ideal for situations where you need to frequently update your filtering criteria, such as blocking specific IP addresses or ports.

Creating and Using Named Sets

Here's how you can create and use named sets in NFTables.

Let's say we want to create a set for a group of IP addresses we want to block:

Create a named set for a list of IP addresses to block:

sudo nft add set inet filter blocked_ips { type ipv4_addr \; }

In this example:

We are creating a named set called blocked_ips.

The type ipv4_addr indicates that this set will hold IPv4 addresses.

The set is part of the inet family, which supports both IPv4 and IPv6.

Once the set is created, we can add IP addresses to the set:

Add IP addresses to the blocked set:

sudo nft add element inet filter blocked_ips { 192.168.1.10, 192.168.2.20 }

Now that we have a named set with two IP addresses, we can use this set in a rule to block traffic from these IPs:

Drop traffic from any IP in the blocked_ips set:

sudo nft add rule inet filter input ip saddr @blocked_ips drop

This rule drops any incoming traffic from IP addresses contained in the blocked_ips set. Using a set makes it easy to update the list of blocked IPs.

For example, to add more IPs, you only need to update the set rather than editing multiple rules:

Add another IP to the blocked set:

sudo nft add element inet filter blocked_ips { 192.168.3.30 }

The key benefit of using named sets is that changes to the set automatically propagate to all the rules referencing that set. This centralizes management and reduces the need for individual rule modifications.

Managing Sets Efficiently

You can also manage and list the sets with these commands:

List the contents of the set:

sudo nft list set inet filter blocked_ips

Delete an element from the set:

sudo nft delete element inet filter blocked_ips { 192.168.1.10 }

Named sets in NFTables are efficient because they minimize rule duplication and allow for easy modifications to the set, rather than requiring changes across multiple individual rules.

Advanced Packet Filtering and Classification

NFTables offers advanced capabilities for packet filtering and classification, allowing administrators to create complex and flexible firewall policies. These capabilities enable fine-grained control over network traffic, ensuring that packets are filtered based on a wide range of conditions. In addition to the basic accept or drop actions, NFTables allows you to classify packets and apply advanced filtering based on various attributes such as connection tracking, packet marking, and more.

Packet Classification with Rules and Marks

Packet classification in NFTables is the process of tagging packets with a specific mark or label, which can later be used to apply certain actions or make decisions about how traffic is handled. This is useful for quality of service (QoS), advanced routing decisions, or traffic shaping.

Here's an example of marking packets based on their source address:

Mark packets from a specific IP address with a unique identifier:

```
sudo nft add rule inet filter input ip saddr 192.168.1.10 mark set 1
```

In this example, packets from the IP address 192.168.1.10 are marked with the value 1.

You can then create another rule that takes action based on the mark:

Drop packets with mark 1:

```
sudo nft add rule inet filter input mark 1 drop
```

This rule ensures that all packets marked with 1 will be dropped. Packet marking allows for complex rule creation where certain traffic can be handled differently based on the tags or conditions associated with the packets.

Using Connection Tracking for Advanced Filtering

NFTables integrates with the connection tracking system, which tracks the state of network connections (such as new, established, or related). This allows for stateful packet filtering, where rules can depend on the state of a connection.

For example, to allow established connections and related traffic while dropping new traffic:

Allow established and related connections:

sudo nft add rule inet filter input ct state established,related accept

Drop new incoming connections:

sudo nft add rule inet filter input ct state new drop

This configuration ensures that only packets related to already established connections are allowed, while new, unsolicited connections are blocked. This is commonly used in firewall setups to protect against unsolicited inbound traffic.

Rate Limiting and Traffic Control

NFTables also supports rate limiting, which allows you to control the rate at which packets are accepted or dropped.

For example, to limit SSH connections to a certain rate (e.g., no more than 3 connections per minute from a single IP), you can use the limit match extension:

Limit SSH connections to 3 per minute per IP:

sudo nft add rule inet filter input tcp dport 22 limit rate 3/minute accept

This rule will limit the rate of incoming SSH connections to 3 per minute from each IP address. If an IP exceeds this limit, further connections will be dropped.

Using NFTables with Queues for Traffic Processing

NFTables also supports integrating with other traffic control tools, such as **tc** (traffic control) and iptables-based queuing mechanisms. This allows for complex packet processing that can be used for shaping, marking, or redirecting traffic based on detailed conditions.

For example, a rule could be set up to direct specific traffic (based on IP, port, or protocol) into a queue for processing by a traffic shaping tool:

Send all HTTP traffic to a specific queue for shaping:

sudo nft add rule inet filter input tcp dport 80 queue 1

This command routes all HTTP traffic into the queue 1, where it can be processed by traffic shaping tools, enabling advanced network management features like bandwidth throttling.

Chapter 11: Managing Network Address Translation (NAT) in NFTables

Network Address Translation (NAT) is a critical function for managing IP address mapping and traffic routing in many network configurations. NAT is often used to allow multiple devices on a local network to share a single public IP address when accessing the internet. This chapter covers how to configure NAT in NFTables, focusing on port forwarding, masquerading, and the performance improvements in NFTables compared to IPtables.

Configuring NAT in NFTables

NFTables supports several types of NAT, including source NAT (SNAT), destination NAT (DNAT), and masquerading. These operations allow you to modify the source or destination address of network packets, providing important routing and security benefits.

In NFTables, NAT is configured within the nat table. The nat table is specifically designed for handling address translation, and it contains chains that are invoked at different points in the packet flow.

Creating the NAT Table

To get started with NAT in NFTables, you first need to create the nat table:

Create a nat table for NAT operations (SNAT, DNAT, Masquerading):

sudo nft add table inet nat

The inet family is typically used to support both IPv4 and IPv6, but you can also create specific IPv4 (ip) or IPv6 (ip6) tables if necessary. Once the table is created, you can proceed to define chains and rules for different NAT operations.

Port Forwarding and Masquerading

Port Forwarding with DNAT

Port forwarding is a form of Destination NAT (DNAT), where incoming traffic on a specific port is forwarded to a different internal IP address and port. This is often used for web servers, SSH servers, or any service that needs to be publicly accessible.

For example, to forward incoming HTTP traffic (port 80) to an internal server with IP 192.168.1.10, you can use the following rule:

Forward incoming HTTP traffic (port 80) to internal server 192.168.1.10:

```
sudo nft add rule inet nat prerouting tcp dport 80 dnat
to 192.168.1.10:80
```

In this example:

prerouting is the chain where DNAT is applied. This occurs when the packet is first received by the router.

The rule matches packets with a destination port of 80 and forwards them to the internal server at IP 192.168.1.10.

Similarly, you can forward traffic for other services like SSH (port 22) to an internal machine:

Forward incoming SSH traffic (port 22) to internal server 192.168.1.20:

```
sudo nft add rule inet nat prerouting tcp dport 22 dnat to 192.168.1.20:22
```

Masquerading for Outbound Traffic (SNAT)

Masquerading is a form of Source NAT (SNAT) commonly used when a private network shares a single public IP address. This is especially useful for home or office routers where the private internal network uses local IP addresses (e.g., 192.168.x.x), but outbound traffic appears to come from the router's public IP.

To enable masquerading for a network interface (e.g., eth0), you would add a rule like this:

Enable Masquerading for outbound traffic:

```
sudo nft add rule inet nat postrouting oifname "eth0" masquerade
```

In this example:

The rule is added to the postrouting chain, which is applied after the packet has been routed.

oifname "eth0" specifies that the rule applies to packets leaving through the eth0 interface.

masquerade modifies the source IP of outgoing packets to the public IP address of the eth0 interface.

Masquerading is ideal when the public IP of the router is dynamically assigned by an ISP (e.g., using DHCP), as it automatically ensures that the source address of the packets is updated to match the current public IP.

NAT Performance Improvements in NFTables vs. IPtables

One of the significant advantages of NFTables over IPtables is its improved performance, particularly in handling NAT operations. NFTables was designed with performance in mind, addressing some of the limitations found in IPtables, especially as networks grow larger and more complex.

Efficient Rule Handling with the Netlink Interface

NFTables utilizes the Netlink interface, a more efficient and modern method for communicating with the kernel compared to the older iptables mechanism. This results in fewer system calls and better overall performance when adding or removing rules.

With IPtables, each new rule could lead to the re-evaluation of every rule in the chain, which could cause performance degradation, especially when handling a large number of rules. In contrast, NFTables processes rules in a more optimized manner, using a single rule set per chain and hash tables for fast lookups.

Better State Management

NFTables includes better integration with connection tracking (conntrack), which tracks the state of network connections. This allows for more efficient stateful packet filtering and NAT, reducing the need for repeated evaluations of the same connection state and improving performance.

In IPtables, connection tracking could become cumbersome when handling a large volume of traffic, as rules would need to be evaluated repeatedly for each packet. NFTables optimizes this by keeping track of the connection state more efficiently, making it less resource-intensive.

Optimized for Modern Hardware

NFTables has been designed with modern hardware in mind, taking advantage of advancements in hardware offloading and hardware packet processing. This allows NFTables to handle large amounts of traffic with minimal CPU overhead, which is particularly useful for high-performance servers and routers.

Simplified Rule Set Management

NFTables also simplifies the rule management process. IPtables required the creation of multiple tables (e.g., filter, nat, mangle), which could sometimes result in complex and cumbersome rule sets. NFTables consolidates this into a more unified structure, reducing the complexity of rule management and improving performance by streamlining rule evaluation.

Chapter 12: Logging, Monitoring, and Debugging NFTables

Effective logging, monitoring, and debugging are essential for maintaining the security and functionality of your firewall configuration. In this chapter, we'll cover how to create logging rules in NFTables, monitor the firewall rules in action, and debug any misconfigurations. This chapter is particularly relevant to Debian systems, where logs are handled by systemd's journal, which provides an efficient way to track and analyze log entries.

Creating Logging Rules for Traffic Analysis

Logging is a critical component of any security system as it allows you to track and analyze network traffic for anomalies, intrusions, or misconfigurations. In NFTables, logging rules help capture packet data for review without affecting the flow of traffic itself.

Debian systems use journalctl to access logs. By default, NFTables logs are written to the system journal, which can be viewed using journal commands.

Adding a Basic Logging Rule

To create a logging rule in NFTables, you can use the log target to capture traffic that matches a specific condition.

For instance, if you want to log all incoming SSH traffic on port 22, you can add a logging rule to the input chain:

sudo nft add rule inet filter input tcp dport 22 log prefix "SSH Attempt: " group 0

In this example:

log: This action tells NFTables to log matching packets.

prefix: You can add a custom string, such as "SSH Attempt: ", to identify these log entries.

group 0: Defines the log group for organization. Group 0 is commonly used for general traffic.

Logging Dropped Packets

It's common to log packets that are dropped for later analysis.

For example, to log and drop all packets that don't match a set of rules, use the following rule:

```
sudo nft add rule inet filter input log drop
```

This rule logs all incoming traffic that does not match previous rules and then drops the packet. It provides insight into potential attack vectors or misconfigurations.

Using syslog for Detailed Logs

Debian systems use **systemd's journal** by default for logging. When you add logging rules in NFTables, log entries are written to the journal, which you can access using the journalctl command.

To view the logs for SSH attempts, use:

sudo journalctl -t nftables | grep "SSH Attempt:"

This command filters out logs related to SSH attempts from the system journal, allowing you to quickly monitor specific traffic types.

Monitoring NFTables Rules in Action

Monitoring your NFTables firewall rules is crucial to ensure that traffic flows according to your intended configuration. It helps identify any unexpected behavior and offers a real-time view of the traffic being filtered.

Viewing Active Rules

You can list the active rules in your NFTables configuration using the following command:

sudo nft list ruleset

This will display the entire set of rules, chains, and tables currently loaded in your system. It provides an overview of all the active filtering rules in NFTables.

For example, you might see something like this:

```
table inet filter {
    chain input {
        type filter hook input priority 0; policy drop;
        tcp dport ssh accept
        log prefix "SSH Attempt: " group 0
        drop
    }
    chain forward {
        type filter hook forward priority 0; policy drop;
        drop
    }
}
```

Real-Time Traffic Monitoring with nft

NFTables allows you to monitor packet flows in real-time using the nft command. This can help you verify that traffic is being filtered according to the rules you've set.

```
sudo nft monitor
```

The nft monitor command shows real-time traffic matching your rules. For example, it can display a log of all packets being accepted, dropped, or logged as they match your rules.

Using journalctl to View NFTables Logs

As mentioned earlier, Debian uses systemd's journal for logging.

To view logs for NFTables traffic, you can use:

sudo journalctl -t nftables

This shows all log entries associated with NFTables rules. By combining the logging functionality of NFTables with journalctl, you can effectively monitor traffic, detect unusual activity, and ensure your firewall is operating as expected.

Debugging Rule Misconfigurations

Misconfigurations in firewall rules can lead to blocked legitimate traffic, security holes, or degraded network performance. Debugging NFTables rule misconfigurations involves examining the rule set, checking logs, and ensuring that rules are applied correctly.

Checking for Syntax and Rule Errors

Before troubleshooting, ensure that the syntax of your NFTables commands is correct.

Use the following command to check the current ruleset for errors:

sudo nft list ruleset

If you suspect an issue with a particular chain, you can isolate the problem by disabling certain rules or chains and gradually enabling them again to pinpoint the misconfiguration.

Review Logs for Dropped or Rejected Traffic

If packets are being unexpectedly dropped, you can review the logs to see what traffic is being rejected. For example, if you've configured a rule to log dropped packets, check the logs with:

sudo journalctl -t nftables | grep "Dropped"

This command filters for logs where packets have been dropped, providing insights into potential misconfigurations, such as accidentally blocking traffic that should be allowed.

Test Rules with nft Commands

NFTables has built-in testing features that allow you to simulate how packets are processed by your rules.

For instance, you can test whether a packet matches a particular rule with:

```
sudo nft -t inet filter -A input -p tcp --dport 80 -j ACCEPT
```

To see if a particular rule is being applied correctly to packets, you can simulate a packet match with:

```
sudo nft list ruleset
```

This command displays the active ruleset, and you can adjust rules or log output to troubleshoot traffic flow issues.

Check Network Interface Configuration

If traffic is not being processed as expected, ensure that the correct network interface is configured in your NFTables rules.

For example, if you are performing NAT or masquerading, make sure the rule specifies the correct interface:

```
sudo nft add rule inet nat postrouting oifname "eth0" masquerade
```

Verify that eth0 is indeed the correct interface in your system. You can list interfaces using the ip link command:

```
ip link show
```

Using nft Debugging Tools

NFTables includes a debug option that can help you identify issues with specific rules or chains.

For example, to enable debugging for specific rule sets, you can add the following to your rule:

```
sudo nft add rule inet filter input ip saddr 192.168.1.10 log prefix "Debugging: "
```

This rule logs any incoming packets from the IP 192.168.1.10, which can help you trace traffic from a specific source.

Part 4: Using UFW for Simplified Firewall Management

Chapter 13: Introduction to UFW (Uncomplicated Firewall)

What is UFW and Why It's Easier for Beginners?

UFW (Uncomplicated Firewall) is a front-end tool for managing firewall rules in Linux systems. It was developed to simplify the process of configuring firewall rules, making it more accessible to beginners who may find traditional firewall management tools like iptables or nftables too complex. While iptables and nftables offer robust and flexible control over network traffic, they can be intimidating for new users due to their detailed syntax and configuration options. UFW abstracts much of this complexity, allowing users to set up basic rules with simple commands, making it an ideal solution for most users who want to secure their Linux systems without delving into intricate firewall configuration.

Installing UFW on Different Linux Distributions

UFW is typically included in the default repositories of most major Linux distributions. To install UFW, follow the instructions for your specific distribution.

Installing UFW on Ubuntu/Debian-based Systems:

sudo apt update

sudo apt install ufw

Installing UFW on Fedora/CentOS/RHEL Systems

For CentOS or RHEL systems, you may need to enable EPEL (Extra Packages for Enterprise Linux) first:

sudo dnf install epel-release

sudo dnf install ufw

Installing UFW on Arch Linux:

sudo pacman -S ufw

Once installed, you can enable UFW and begin configuring it.

UFW vs. IPtables and NFTables: Simplifying Firewall Management

UFW is designed to simplify the complexity of working with iptables and nftables. While iptables and nftables offer more granular control over firewall rules and are powerful tools for system administrators, they can be difficult for beginners to manage.

UFW simplifies firewall management by providing simple command-line options for allowing or blocking traffic.

IPtables and NFTables require an understanding of concepts like chains, tables, and rules, and have more complex syntax.

UFW acts as a user-friendly wrapper for iptables, and while it does not offer the same level of fine-tuned control, it is often more than enough for most users who want to manage basic firewall configurations effectively.

Chapter 14: Configuring Basic Rules in UFW

Allowing and Denying Traffic with Simple Commands

One of UFW's key advantages is its simplicity in allowing or denying traffic using very straightforward commands.

Allowing Traffic

To allow incoming traffic on a specific port, such as SSH (port 22), use the following command:

sudo ufw allow 22

You can also specify the protocol (TCP/UDP) if needed:

sudo ufw allow 22/tcp # Allow TCP traffic on port 22 (SSH)

Similarly, to allow HTTP (port 80) traffic:

sudo ufw allow 80/tcp

Denying Traffic

To deny traffic to a particular port, such as blocking HTTP (port 80), use:

sudo ufw deny 80/tcp

You can also block incoming traffic from specific IP addresses:

sudo ufw deny from 192.168.1.10

Checking UFW Status

You can check the current status of UFW and see which rules are active by using:

sudo ufw status

Deleting Rules

If you need to remove a rule, you can use the delete command. For example, to delete the rule allowing SSH:

sudo ufw delete allow 22

Enabling UFW and Setting Default Policies

UFW is disabled by default, so you'll need to enable it after configuring your firewall rules.

Enabling UFW

To enable UFW, use:

sudo ufw enable

Once enabled, UFW will begin enforcing the firewall rules you've configured.

Setting Default Policies

UFW allows you to define default policies for incoming and outgoing traffic. By default, UFW sets the incoming policy to deny and the outgoing policy to allow. This means that all incoming traffic is blocked by default, and all outgoing traffic is allowed.

To confirm or modify these default policies, you can use the following commands:

Set default incoming policy to deny (blocks incoming traffic by default):

sudo ufw default deny incoming

Set default outgoing policy to allow (allows outgoing traffic by default):

sudo ufw default allow outgoing

These default policies help ensure that no traffic can enter the system unless explicitly allowed, enhancing the security of your system.

Managing UFW Profiles for Different Network Interfaces

UFW supports different profiles for managing traffic based on network interfaces. For example, if your server has multiple network interfaces, you can apply specific rules to traffic from each interface.

Listing Available Profiles

To view available application profiles, you can run:

sudo ufw app list

Allowing Traffic for an Application Profile

If you have a predefined application profile for SSH, you can use the following command to allow it:

sudo ufw allow OpenSSH

This simplifies the configuration process by using application profiles instead of manually specifying port numbers. UFW will automatically apply the relevant rules based on the profile's predefined settings.

Chapter 15: Advanced UFW Configuration

While UFW is simple to use, it also supports more advanced configurations for users who need additional functionality. In this chapter, we'll explore some of the advanced capabilities of UFW, including application-specific filtering and customizing rules for specific network interfaces.

Application-Specific Filtering (e.g., SSH, HTTP, FTP)

UFW allows for application-specific filtering by using predefined application profiles. These profiles contain a set of rules for common services like SSH, HTTP, and FTP. This simplifies firewall configuration, as it automatically applies the correct ports and protocols for these services.

Allowing SSH Traffic

To allow SSH traffic, you can use the predefined profile:

```
sudo ufw allow OpenSSH
```

This rule allows incoming traffic for SSH without needing to specify port numbers or protocols manually.

Allowing HTTP and HTTPS Traffic

For a web server, you can allow HTTP and HTTPS traffic using the following commands:

```
sudo ufw allow 'Apache Full'
```

This profile allows both HTTP (port 80) and HTTPS (port 443) traffic for the Apache web server.

Allowing FTP Traffic:

If your server needs to support FTP, you can allow FTP traffic with the following:

```
sudo ufw allow FTP
```

Using predefined application profiles not only saves time but also reduces the risk of errors, as the profiles are carefully configured to work with the respective services.

Customizing Rules for Specific Network Interfaces

You may have multiple network interfaces on your server, and you can create UFW rules that apply only to specific interfaces. This is useful in multi-homed systems or when you want to segregate traffic based on the interface.

For example, to allow SSH traffic only on the eth0 interface, you can use:

sudo ufw allow in on eth0 to any port 22 proto tcp

This command allows TCP traffic on port 22 (SSH) only for the eth0 interface, ensuring that SSH access is restricted to that network interface.

Rate Limiting for Protection Against DoS Attacks

Another advanced feature of UFW is rate limiting, which helps protect your server from certain types of attacks, such as brute-force attacks on SSH.

To rate limit SSH connections, use:

sudo ufw limit ssh/tcp

This rule allows SSH connections but limits the rate at which new connections can be made, helping to prevent abuse and reduce the risk of denial-of-service (DoS) attacks.

Rate Limiting and Preventing Brute-Force Attacks

One of the most common types of attacks on networked systems is a brute-force attack, where an attacker attempts to guess login credentials by systematically trying a large number of passwords. Services like SSH are particularly vulnerable to this type of attack, as attackers can attempt multiple login attempts in rapid succession.

UFW provides an effective method for mitigating brute-force attacks using rate limiting. Rate limiting restricts the number of incoming connection attempts from a single IP address within a short period. If the limit is exceeded, the attacker's IP will be temporarily blocked, preventing further login attempts.

Rate Limiting SSH:

To limit the rate of incoming SSH connections, use the limit option in UFW:

```
sudo ufw limit ssh/tcp
```

This command applies rate limiting to incoming TCP connections on port 22 (SSH). By default, UFW allows a limited number of connections within a specified time frame (e.g., 6 connections within 30 seconds). If the limit is exceeded, UFW will block further attempts from the same IP for a short period.

Rate Limiting Other Services:

Similarly, you can rate limit other services like HTTP or FTP:

sudo ufw limit http/tcp

This helps protect your web server from DoS (Denial of Service) attacks that attempt to overwhelm your server with excessive traffic.

Rate limiting helps reduce the likelihood of successful brute-force attempts while allowing legitimate traffic to flow smoothly. This technique is particularly useful in services where frequent login attempts are common, such as SSH or web applications.

Integrating UFW with IPv6

While UFW works seamlessly with IPv4, it also has the ability to manage firewall rules for IPv6 traffic, making it a versatile solution for modern networks that utilize both IPv4 and IPv6 addressing schemes. With the increasing adoption of IPv6, it's important to ensure that your firewall is properly configured to protect both IPv4 and IPv6 traffic.

By default, UFW enables support for both IPv4 and IPv6 when installed on a system with an IPv6 address. However, it's crucial to verify and configure IPv6 rules separately from IPv4 if your network uses both protocols.

Enabling IPv6 Support in UFW:

To confirm that IPv6 support is enabled in UFW, check the configuration file:

sudo nano /etc/default/ufw

Look for the line:

IPV6=yes

If it is set to yes, UFW will manage IPv6 traffic. If you want to disable IPv6 support for any reason, change this setting to no.

Allowing Traffic for IPv6

To allow IPv6 traffic on a specific port, such as HTTP (port 80), you can use:

sudo ufw allow 80/tcp

This rule applies to both IPv4 and IPv6 traffic by default. To specify only IPv6, use the ip6 option:

sudo ufw allow 80/tcp from any to any proto tcp ip6

Similarly, if you need to block IPv6 traffic, you can do so by specifying the IPv6 address or using the ip6 option:

sudo ufw deny from 2001:db8::/32

This will deny traffic from the specified IPv6 subnet.

Verifying IPv6 Rules

You can check the status of your firewall and see which IPv6 rules are applied with:

sudo ufw status

This will list both IPv4 and IPv6 rules, giving you a comprehensive view of the firewall configuration for both protocols.

Properly configuring IPv6 rules is essential as the internet moves toward a dual-stack (IPv4 and IPv6) environment. Ensuring that both protocols are secured can help prevent vulnerabilities in your network.

Chapter 16: Logging, Monitoring, and Troubleshooting UFW

Enabling Logging and Reviewing Firewall Logs

Effective logging is a critical component of firewall management, as it provides insights into the types of traffic being allowed or blocked by your firewall. UFW can log events such as dropped packets, denied connections, and accepted traffic, which helps you monitor and troubleshoot your firewall rules.

Enabling UFW Logging:

By default, UFW logging is disabled. To enable logging, use the following command:

sudo ufw logging on

This enables logging at the default level, which records the most basic information. For more detailed logs, you can adjust the logging level.

Setting the Logging Level

UFW offers several logging levels that determine the amount of information logged. The available levels are:

low: Logs only basic packet information (e.g., denied connections).

medium: Logs more detailed packet information.

high: Logs all traffic, including accepted packets.

full: Logs detailed information about both allowed and denied packets.

To change the logging level, use:

sudo ufw logging high

This command will log all incoming and outgoing traffic, providing a complete view of the firewall activity.

Viewing Firewall Logs:

UFW logs are stored in the system log file, typically located at /var/log/ufw.log.

You can review the logs using standard log viewing tools such as cat, less, or tail:

```
sudo less /var/log/ufw.log
```

Alternatively, you can view real-time logs with:

```
sudo tail -f /var/log/ufw.log
```

These logs will show you the firewall's activity, including allowed and denied traffic, which can be useful for troubleshooting and auditing.

Common Troubleshooting Techniques for UFW

While UFW is relatively easy to configure, issues may arise when incorrect or conflicting rules are applied.

Checking UFW Status

If you're unsure about your current firewall configuration, use:

```
sudo ufw status verbose
```

This will show you detailed information about the active rules, default policies, and logging settings.

Checking for Rule Conflicts

If you have conflicting rules, UFW may not behave as expected. Use the status command to ensure no contradictory rules are present. For example, check if both allow and deny rules exist for the same port, which could cause unpredictable results.

Resetting UFW Rules

If troubleshooting becomes too complex or confusing, you can reset UFW to its default state:

sudo ufw reset

This command clears all current rules and restores UFW to its default configuration.

Testing Specific Rules

You can test a specific rule by attempting to access a service that is either allowed or denied, using a tool like curl or nc to simulate network requests. This helps you verify whether the rule is functioning as intended.

Debugging UFW Rule Conflicts

Rule conflicts typically occur when multiple rules affect the same service or IP address. UFW's logging feature can help you identify these conflicts by showing the traffic that is being allowed or denied.

Identifying Conflicting Rules:

Look for logs that indicate blocked traffic that should have been allowed, or vice versa. For example, if you have a rule allowing SSH but still see it being blocked, it may indicate a conflicting deny rule.

Prioritizing Rules:

UFW processes rules sequentially, with the first matching rule being applied. To avoid conflicts, ensure that more specific rules are placed before more general ones. For instance, if you have a general rule blocking all incoming traffic, make sure specific rules (e.g., allowing SSH) are listed above it.

Using ufw status numbered:

For further troubleshooting, you can use ufw status numbered to view rules with assigned numbers. If necessary, you can delete specific rules by their number:

sudo ufw delete 2

This is useful when you need to remove a conflicting rule that is difficult to identify by its description.

Part 5: Practical Use Cases and Security Best Practices

Chapter 17: Building a Secure Home Network Firewall

A home network firewall is crucial for protecting personal devices and ensuring the safety of your internet connection. While home routers often come with basic firewall functionalities, setting up a more robust and customizable firewall with tools like IPtables and UFW can provide a higher level of security.

Setting Up a Basic Firewall for Home Use with IPtables and UFW

For a simple home firewall, UFW (Uncomplicated Firewall) is an excellent choice because it's easy to configure, even for beginners.

Install UFW

On most Linux systems, UFW can be installed easily using the following command:

sudo apt install ufw

Enable UFW and set default policies

First, set default policies to deny all incoming connections and allow outgoing traffic:

sudo ufw default deny incoming

sudo ufw default allow outgoing

Allow necessary services

Next, allow common services like HTTP (80/tcp) and SSH (22/tcp) for remote administration:

sudo ufw allow ssh

sudo ufw allow http

Enable the firewall

Finally, enable the firewall:

sudo ufw enable

This configuration sets up a basic home network firewall that allows web browsing and remote access via SSH while blocking all other incoming traffic.

Securing Common Services like SSH and HTTP

While SSH and HTTP are essential services, they are common targets for attackers.

To enhance their security

For SSH, limit access to trusted IPs:

sudo ufw allow from <trusted_IP> to any port 22

For HTTP, restrict access to specific IPs for admin or management purposes:

sudo ufw allow from <trusted_IP> to any port 80

Additionally, ensure SSH uses strong authentication methods like key-based login rather than passwords.

Preventing Unauthorized Access to Your Home Network

Enable logging to monitor access attempts:

sudo ufw logging on

Rate limit incoming connections to prevent brute-force attacks:

sudo ufw limit ssh/tcp

This setup will significantly reduce the risk of unauthorized access to your home network, while allowing you to manage network traffic efficiently.

Chapter 18: Securing a Web Server

A web server is often the target of various attacks, such as DDoS (Distributed Denial of Service) or SQL injection. Therefore, securing your web server's firewall is essential for ensuring the safety of your website and its data.

Firewall Rules for Web Hosting: Securing HTTP/HTTPS Traffic

When hosting a website, you need to allow HTTP (port 80) and HTTPS (port 443) traffic while denying all other incoming connections.

You can configure this using IPtables or UFW

Allow HTTP and HTTPS traffic:

With UFW, you can allow these ports with:

sudo ufw allow http

sudo ufw allow https

Block unnecessary services:

Ensure that other ports (such as FTP or SSH) are blocked unless specifically required:

sudo ufw deny ftp

sudo ufw deny ssh

Protecting Your Server Against DDoS Attacks

DDoS attacks aim to overwhelm your server with excessive traffic. You can mitigate DDoS attacks using rate limiting and connection tracking to limit the impact of these attacks.

Rate limiting with UFW

Limit the number of incoming connections to HTTP and HTTPS:

sudo ufw limit http/tcp

sudo ufw limit https/tcp

Connection tracking

You can enable connection tracking to monitor the state of incoming traffic and block abnormal patterns that suggest a DDoS attack:

sudo sysctl -w net.netfilter.nf_conntrack_max=65536

This helps prevent server overload and ensures only legitimate traffic is processed.

Rate Limiting and Logging for Web Applications

Log HTTP traffic

Use logging to identify attack attempts:

sudo ufw logging high

Monitor traffic patterns:

Regularly check logs for unusual spikes in traffic, which could indicate a DDoS or brute-force attack.

By combining these measures, you ensure that your web server is both protected against external threats and able to provide a reliable service to legitimate users.

Chapter 19: Firewall Rules for VPN and Remote Access

Virtual Private Networks (VPNs) are often used to securely access a network from a remote location. Proper firewall configuration is critical to ensure that VPN services are secure while allowing authorized users to access the network.

Configuring Firewall Rules for VPN Services

Whether you are using OpenVPN, WireGuard, or another VPN service, you need to configure your firewall to allow the necessary ports and protocols while securing the rest of the network.

Allow VPN traffic

For OpenVPN, the default port is UDP 1194:

sudo ufw allow 1194/udp

Allow UDP for WireGuard

If you're using WireGuard, you might configure the firewall to allow traffic on port 51820:

sudo ufw allow 51820/udp

Secure VPN traffic

To ensure security, limit VPN access to trusted IPs or networks. You can also enable logging to monitor VPN usage.

Securing Remote Access via SSH with IPtables/NFTables

For SSH remote access, make sure that the firewall only allows SSH connections from specific IP addresses.

For example:

sudo ufw allow from <trusted_IP> to any port 22

Additionally, use key-based authentication instead of passwords for added security.

Dynamic Firewall Rules for Mobile Devices and Roaming Users

If users connect to your network using mobile devices or frequently change their IP address (e.g., roaming users), setting dynamic firewall rules can help secure their connections. VPN services can provide a secure and stable IP range, ensuring that the firewall can be adjusted dynamically for users who might change their network location.

You can use dynamic IP address blocks or allow IP ranges associated with your VPN provider, ensuring access is granted only to authorized mobile users.

Chapter 20: Performance Optimization and Best Practices

When managing a firewall in a high-traffic environment, it's crucial to optimize performance while maintaining robust security. Inefficient firewall configurations can lead to increased latency, degraded server performance, and slower network speeds.

Optimizing Firewall Performance for High-Traffic Environments

Minimize rules processing: Avoid creating too many rules that may require the firewall to process large volumes of data. Instead, prioritize specific traffic filters.

Use connection tracking efficiently: Connection tracking helps determine the state of a connection and can prevent the firewall from inspecting every packet in an ongoing connection. This is crucial for high-traffic environments where performance is critical.

Use a "whitelist" approach: Rather than allowing traffic from all sources and blocking specific malicious traffic, create rules that allow traffic from trusted sources only.

Using Connection Tracking Efficiently

Efficient connection tracking ensures that the firewall processes only necessary data. This allows for faster decision-making while handling large amounts of network traffic. For example, by enabling TCP connection tracking, the firewall can quickly determine whether incoming traffic is part of an existing connection.

Ensuring Firewall Rules Are Structured for Maintainability and Scalability

Organize rules logically: Structure your firewall rules in a logical order, grouping them by service or protocol, making it easier to troubleshoot and update.

Use comments for clarity: Add comments to your firewall rules to describe their purpose and behavior, making future maintenance easier.

Regular audits: Regularly audit your firewall configuration to ensure it remains effective as your network grows.

Part 6: Automation, Scripting, and Tools

Chapter 21: Automating Firewall Rule Management

Automating firewall rule management is crucial for maintaining a secure, efficient, and responsive system, especially as your infrastructure grows or changes frequently. By using scripts and scheduling tools, administrators can minimize the time spent on manual rule updates, ensure consistency, and quickly adapt to new requirements.

Using Bash Scripts for Dynamic Rule Generation

Bash scripting allows you to automate the creation of firewall rules dynamically. For example, you might need to allow or deny traffic based on real-time IP addresses or services.

Here's an example script that automatically adds an IP address to the firewall blocklist when it is flagged for suspicious activity:

```bash
#!/bin/bash

# Variables
IP_ADDRESS=$1

# Check if the IP address is provided
if [ -z "$IP_ADDRESS" ]; then
  echo "Please provide an IP address to block."
  exit 1
fi
# Add the IP to the blacklist using IPtables

sudo iptables -A INPUT -s $IP_ADDRESS -j DROP

echo "$IP_ADDRESS has been blocked."
```

This script takes an IP address as input, then uses iptables to drop all traffic from that IP. It can be adapted to check for specific traffic patterns and add dynamic rules as needed.

Automating Firewall Rule Updates with Cron Jobs

cron is a time-based job scheduler in Unix-like operating systems. It can be used to automate regular tasks, such as updating firewall rules, cleaning up old log files, or rotating configuration backups.

For example, if you need to automatically update the firewall every night at midnight to apply any changes made

to a list of allowed IP addresses, you can schedule a cron job:

Open the cron file for editing:

crontab -e

Add a cron job to run the firewall update script every night:

0 0 * * * /path/to/update_firewall.sh

This example runs update_firewall.sh at midnight every day, ensuring that the firewall configuration is always up-to-date.

Tools for Managing Large Rule Sets Efficiently:

As the number of firewall rules grows, managing them manually becomes cumbersome.

There are several tools and approaches that help automate and efficiently manage large rule sets:

Firewalld: A dynamic firewall manager for Linux systems, Firewalld uses zones and services to manage rules. It abstracts the complex rule configuration into simpler settings.

Ansible: Ansible is an automation tool that can be used to manage firewall rules across multiple servers. With Ansible, you can define firewall rules as part of your infrastructure-as-code setup.

NFTables Management Tools: Tools like nft allow administrators to manage complex rule sets using a more straightforward syntax than iptables.

Example of using Ansible to apply firewall rules across multiple machines:

```
- name: Apply firewall rules
hosts: all
tasks:
- name: Add rule to allow SSH traffic
ufw:
rule: allow
name: ssh
state: enabled
```

Using such tools ensures that large-scale firewall management remains efficient and scalable.

Chapter 22: Integrating Firewalls with Security Tools

Firewalls are essential for securing a network, but integrating them with other security tools further enhances protection. By combining firewalls with systems like IDS/IPS, Fail2ban, and security auditing tools, you can improve threat detection, automatic responses, and ongoing system verification.

IDS/IPS (Intrusion Detection/Prevention Systems) Integration

An IDS (Intrusion Detection System) monitors network traffic for suspicious activity, while an IPS (Intrusion Prevention System) takes action to block that activity. Integrating these systems with your firewall adds an additional layer of security.

For example, integrating Snort, an open-source IDS/IPS, with your firewall allows you to identify and block malicious traffic before it reaches your critical systems. You could configure Snort to send alerts or trigger automatic firewall updates when it detects certain threats.

Here's a simplified example using iptables to block an IP address after Snort detects suspicious traffic:

Snort detects an attack.

A script is triggered to block the source IP using iptables:

```
iptables -A INPUT -s <attacker_ip> -j DROP
```

This integration ensures that once an attack is detected, it is immediately neutralized at the firewall level.

Using Fail2ban with IPtables/NFTables/UFW to Block Brute-Force Attacks

Fail2ban is a popular tool used to prevent brute-force attacks by scanning log files for multiple failed login attempts and automatically blocking the offending IP addresses.

Here's an example configuration for using Fail2ban with UFW to block SSH brute-force attacks:

Install Fail2ban:

```
sudo apt install fail2ban
```

Configure Fail2ban for SSH

Create a local configuration file /etc/fail2ban/jail.local:

```
[ssh]
enabled = true
port = ssh
filter = sshd
logpath = /var/log/auth.log
maxretry = 3
bantime = 600
action = ufw[block]
```

Restart Fail2ban:

sudo systemctl restart fail2ban

In this configuration, if an IP fails 3 login attempts within a short period, it will be blocked for 10 minutes.

Security Auditing Tools for Firewall Testing and Verification

Tools like Nmap, Nessus, and OpenVAS can be used to test your firewall's effectiveness and ensure that the firewall is properly configured.

For example, using Nmap, you can scan your firewall to check for open ports:

nmap -p 22,80,443 <server_ip>

This command checks whether SSH (22), HTTP (80), and HTTPS (443) ports are open. You can use this to verify whether your firewall is correctly blocking unrequested ports.

OpenVAS is another comprehensive vulnerability scanner that can test firewall misconfigurations and expose any weaknesses in your network security.

Chapter 23: Troubleshooting Common Firewall Issues

Proper troubleshooting techniques are essential to ensure that firewall misconfigurations are detected and resolved quickly, minimizing the impact of any potential security breaches.

Diagnosing and Fixing Misconfigured Rules

Common firewall misconfigurations include accidentally blocking essential services, allowing unwanted traffic, or ordering rules incorrectly.

Use the iptables -L command to list current firewall rules:

sudo iptables -L -v

Check for blocked services

If a service (such as SSH) is not working, it could be blocked by the firewall. Ensure that the necessary ports are open:

sudo iptables -A INPUT -p tcp --dport 22 -j ACCEPT

Check for conflicting rules: Sometimes, conflicting rules can cause issues. For instance, a rule denying all traffic might inadvertently block more than intended. Check the rule order and ensure specific allow rules are placed above any general deny rules.

Dealing with Firewall-Related Performance Bottlenecks

Firewalls can introduce performance bottlenecks if they are not optimized. For example, using overly broad or unnecessary rules can lead to slower network performance.

To diagnose performance issues:

Check system performance using top or htop to monitor CPU usage and memory consumption.

Optimize rules by removing unnecessary rules or condensing similar ones. Use connection tracking efficiently to avoid overburdening the firewall.

Measure latency with ping or traceroute to identify if the firewall is causing network delays.

Ensuring Firewall Rules Survive System Reboots

After a system reboot, firewall rules can be lost unless they are saved properly. To ensure that firewall rules persist across reboots, you can use the following commands:

For IPtables:

sudo iptables-save > /etc/iptables/rules.v4

Then, ensure that IPtables is restored on boot by configuring it in /etc/network/if-up.d/iptables.

For UFW, simply enable it:

sudo ufw enable

This ensures that your firewall rules are automatically reapplied after a reboot.

Part 7: Advanced Topics

Chapter 24: Firewalling in Virtualized and Containerized

The rise of virtualization and containerization has significantly altered the landscape of IT infrastructure. In these environments, firewalls play an essential role in isolating and securing different workloads and network interfaces. This chapter explores how to manage firewalls in virtualized and containerized environments, focusing on Docker, Kubernetes, KVM, QEMU, and network namespaces.

Managing Firewalls in Docker Containers and Kubernetes Clusters

Containerization platforms like Docker and Kubernetes rely on networking technologies to isolate containers and facilitate communication between them. Managing firewall rules in these environments requires a slightly different approach compared to traditional server setups.

Docker Containers:

By default, Docker uses a bridge network driver, which assigns each container its own virtual network interface. Docker configures firewall rules automatically when containers are launched, but you can also manage firewall rules manually using iptables or nftables.

Listing Docker-created iptables rules

Docker modifies iptables to create custom rules for container networking. You can view them using:

sudo iptables -t filter -L -n

Manually adding rules

You can specify custom firewall rules to control traffic to and from containers. For example, to allow SSH access to a container, you might add:

sudo iptables -A DOCKER-USER -s <container_ip> -p tcp --dport 22 -j ACCEPT

Kubernetes Clusters

Kubernetes provides network policies to control traffic between pods, but these policies are not firewalls in the traditional sense. You can integrate Kubernetes with external firewalls or use network policies to manage intra-cluster traffic.

To create a simple network policy in Kubernetes:

```
apiVersion: networking.k8s.io/v1
kind: NetworkPolicy
metadata:
name: allow-only-http
spec:
podSelector: {}
ingress:
- from:
- podSelector: {}
ports:
- protocol: TCP
port: 80
```

This policy allows incoming HTTP traffic on port 80 to all pods. In a more complex scenario, you can combine Kubernetes network policies with host-level firewalls (using iptables or nftables) for enhanced security.

Firewall Rules for Virtual Machines using KVM and QEMU

Virtual machines (VMs) created with KVM (Kernel-based Virtual Machine) and QEMU (Quick Emulator) require careful firewall management to ensure secure traffic between the host and guest systems.

Managing Virtual Network Interfaces: KVM/QEMU typically creates virtual network interfaces (such as virbr0) for the VMs. You can manage traffic to and from these interfaces using traditional firewall tools.

Example to allow HTTP access to a VM:

sudo iptables -A FORWARD -d <vm_ip> -p tcp --dport 80 -j ACCEPT

NAT and Port Forwarding: If the VM is using NAT (Network Address Translation), you may need to configure port forwarding rules to allow access to specific services.

For instance:

sudo iptables -t nat -A PREROUTING -p tcp --dport 8080 -j DNAT --to-destination <vm_ip>:80

Isolating VMs

If you want to isolate VMs and prevent communication between them, you can block internal traffic using:

sudo iptables -A FORWARD -i virbr0 -o virbr0 -j DROP

Network Namespaces and Firewalls for Isolated Environments

Network namespaces in Linux allow for the creation of isolated network environments. Each network namespace can have its own routing table, IP addresses, and firewall rules. This makes it possible to create secure, isolated environments for containers or virtual machines.

To create a firewall for a network namespace

Create the network namespace:

sudo ip netns add mynamespace

Attach a virtual interface:

sudo ip link set veth0 netns mynamespace

Apply firewall rules to the namespace:

sudo ip netns exec mynamespace iptables -A INPUT -p tcp --dport 22 -j ACCEPT

Network namespaces combined with firewalls can be useful for building isolated environments within a single machine, ensuring that traffic between namespaces is strictly controlled.

Chapter 25: IPv6 Firewalling

The adoption of IPv6 introduces new complexities for firewalling, as IPv6 provides a much larger address space and introduces different networking principles compared to IPv4. This chapter explores how to handle firewall rules for IPv6 traffic using iptables, nftables, and UFW.

IPv6 Basics and the Need for IPv6 Firewalls

IPv6 provides an almost unlimited address space, allowing for the unique addressing of each device in a network. However, with this increased address space comes the need for new firewall rules, as the address range for IPv6 is much larger than IPv4, which could make unauthorized traffic more difficult to track.

Some key features of IPv6 include:

Stateless Address Autoconfiguration (SLAAC): Devices can automatically configure their own IP addresses.

No NAT: Unlike IPv4, IPv6 does not require NAT (Network Address Translation), which can simplify firewalling but also requires more precise access control.

Writing IPtables, NFTables, and UFW Rules for IPv6

To configure IPv6 firewalling, you can use either iptables or nftables. The configuration for IPv6 is similar to IPv4, but you need to ensure you're specifying IPv6 addresses and protocols.

IPtables (IPv6)

To allow incoming HTTP traffic over IPv6:

sudo ip6tables -A INPUT -p tcp --dport 80 -j ACCEPT

NFTables (IPv6)

With nftables, you can write more flexible rules for IPv6 traffic:

nft add rule inet filter input ip6 daddr <ipv6_address> tcp dport 80 accept

UFW (IPv6)

To enable IPv6 in UFW and allow specific traffic:

Ensure UFW is configured for IPv6:

sudo ufw allow from any to any port 80 proto tcp

Enable UFW for IPv6:

sudo ufw enable

Ensuring Dual-Stack Network Security

A dual-stack network supports both IPv4 and IPv6. To ensure security, you must configure your firewall to support both protocols. This typically means setting up separate rules for each, ensuring there are no gaps that attackers could exploit.

For example, you can add IPv6-specific rules in addition to your existing IPv4 rules:

sudo iptables -A INPUT -p tcp --dport 443 -j ACCEPT

sudo ip6tables -A INPUT -p tcp --dport 443 -j ACCEPT

By securing both IPv4 and IPv6 traffic, you ensure that both address spaces are equally protected.

Chapter 26: Future of Linux Firewalls

The world of network security is always evolving, and so are the technologies used to secure Linux systems. This chapter looks at the future of Linux firewalls, the challenges posed by emerging threats, and new firewall technologies that are shaping the future of network security.

What's Next After IPtables and NFTables?

While iptables and nftables remain the standard tools for managing firewalls on Linux, there are emerging technologies that might take over in the future.

For instance:

BPF (eBPF): eBPF (extended Berkeley Packet Filter) allows for more efficient and flexible network filtering. It operates at a lower level than traditional firewalls and can provide highly efficient packet processing and filtering.

Service Meshes: In containerized environments, service meshes like Istio or Linkerd provide sophisticated network traffic management and security features, including encryption, traffic routing, and access control, often replacing traditional firewalls for microservices.

Evolving Threats and How Firewalls Must Adapt

As cybersecurity threats become more sophisticated, firewalls must evolve to address new attack vectors. Some emerging threats include:

Advanced Persistent Threats (APTs): These long-term, targeted attacks are harder to detect and block, requiring more intelligent firewall rules that can adapt to evolving tactics.

IoT Security: With more devices connecting to the internet, firewalls need to account for the unique traffic patterns of IoT devices, often deploying more granular access control policies.

Emerging Firewall Technologies and Trends

Some promising trends and technologies in firewalling include:

AI-Powered Firewalls: Leveraging machine learning algorithms to automatically adjust firewall rules based on network behavior and traffic analysis.

Zero Trust Security: The zero-trust model assumes that every connection, whether inside or outside the network, should be treated as untrusted. This paradigm shift requires firewalls to support more granular access control and continuous monitoring.

Cloud-Native Firewalls: As more companies move to cloud-based infrastructure, firewalls need to operate efficiently in hybrid and multi-cloud environments, offering centralized management of distributed firewall rules.

Appendices

Appendix A: IPtables Cheat Sheet

IPtables is one of the most commonly used tools for firewall management on Linux systems. This cheat sheet provides a quick reference guide to frequently used IPtables commands and options for managing firewall rules.

Basic IPtables Command Structure:

iptables [OPTIONS] [CHAIN] [RULES]

OPTIONS: Commands like -A (Append), -I (Insert), -D (Delete), -L (List), -F (Flush).

CHAIN: The chain where rules are added (e.g., INPUT, OUTPUT, FORWARD).

RULES: Define the rule, such as protocol, source/destination, ports, etc.

Common Commands

List Rules:

sudo iptables -L

Allow Incoming HTTP Traffic:

sudo iptables -A INPUT -p tcp --dport 80 -j ACCEPT

Block All Incoming Traffic:

sudo iptables -P INPUT DROP

Allow SSH (Port 22):

sudo iptables -A INPUT -p tcp --dport 22 -j ACCEPT

Delete a Rule:

sudo iptables -D INPUT -p tcp --dport 80 -j ACCEPT

Save Rules:

sudo iptables-save > /etc/iptables/rules.v4

Flush All Rules:

sudo iptables -F

Block an IP Address:

sudo iptables -A INPUT -s 192.168.1.100 -j DROP

Appendix B: NFTables Syntax Reference

NFTables is the successor to IPtables, designed to offer better performance and flexibility. This reference provides essential syntax for managing firewall rules with nft.

Basic NFTables Command Structure:

nft [OPTIONS] [CHAIN] [RULES]

OPTIONS: Similar to IPtables commands (-a for append, -d for delete, etc.).

CHAIN: The table or chain where the rule applies (e.g., filter, nat, inet).

RULES: Define the rule criteria such as protocol, source/destination, ports, etc.

Basic Commands

Create a New Table:

sudo nft add table inet filter

Create a New Chain:

sudo nft add chain inet filter input { type filter hook input priority 0 \; }

Add a Rule to Allow SSH:

sudo nft add rule inet filter input tcp dport 22 accept

List Rules:

sudo nft list ruleset

Delete a Rule:

sudo nft delete rule inet filter input handle 5

Save Rules:

sudo nft list ruleset > /etc/nftables.conf

Flush All Rules:

sudo nft flush ruleset

Block Incoming Traffic from a Specific IP:

```
sudo nft add rule inet filter input ip saddr 192.168.1.100
drop
```

Appendix C: UFW Command Reference

UFW (Uncomplicated Firewall) is a user-friendly front end for managing iptables. This reference provides basic UFW commands for managing firewall rules.

Basic UFW Command Structure

ufw [COMMAND] [OPTIONS]

Basic Commands

Enable UFW:

sudo ufw enable

Disable UFW:

sudo ufw disable

Allow HTTP Traffic:

sudo ufw allow http

Allow SSH (Port 22):

sudo ufw allow ssh

Block Incoming Traffic:

sudo ufw default deny incoming

Allow Incoming Traffic on a Specific Port:

sudo ufw allow 8080/tcp

Show UFW Status:

sudo ufw status

Delete a Rule:

sudo ufw delete allow 8080/tcp

Allow Access from a Specific IP Address:

sudo ufw allow from 192.168.1.100 to any port 80

Appendix D: Troubleshooting Checklist

This checklist will help you diagnose and resolve common issues with firewalls and network connectivity.

Check Firewall Status:

Ensure the firewall service is running (IPtables, NFTables, or UFW).

Example: sudo systemctl status ufw or sudo systemctl status iptables.

Verify Active Rules:

List the current firewall rules to identify misconfigurations.

Example: sudo iptables -L or sudo nft list ruleset.

Test Connectivity:

Use ping or traceroute to verify if the network is reachable.

Example: ping <destination_IP>.

Check for Blocked Ports:

Ensure required ports are open in the firewall for services (e.g., HTTP, SSH).

Example: sudo ufw status or sudo iptables -L -v.

Confirm IP Addressing and Routing:

Ensure the correct IP address and network interface are configured.

Use ip addr show or ifconfig to check network interfaces.

Review Logs for Errors:

Check firewall logs to identify denied traffic or misconfigurations.

Logs can be found in /var/log/ufw.log, /var/log/kern.log, or /var/log/messages

Or with: sudo journalctl SYSLOG_IDENTIFIER=ufw

Check for Conflicting Rules:

Verify that no rules are conflicting (e.g., a DROP rule overriding ACCEPT).

Review the rule order in iptables or nftables.

Test Services:

Ensure the service behind the firewall is active and correctly configured.

Use sudo systemctl status <service_name> to check service status.

Appendix E: Glossary of Networking and Firewall Terms

This glossary provides definitions for key networking and firewall terms commonly used throughout the guide.

ACL (Access Control List)

A set of rules that defines which users or systems are granted access to resources within a network and what actions they are allowed to perform. ACLs can apply to firewalls, routers, and switches to control network traffic and enforce security policies.

NAT (Network Address Translation)

A technique used to modify IP address information in packet headers as they traverse a router or firewall. NAT is commonly used to allow multiple devices on a private network to share a single public IP address, improving security by hiding internal IP addresses from external networks.

DDoS (Distributed Denial of Service)

An attack where multiple compromised systems flood a target with network traffic, causing disruption or complete shutdown of the target's services. DDoS attacks are challenging to mitigate because the traffic comes from numerous sources.

Packet Filtering

A process that inspects incoming and outgoing network packets based on pre-configured rules and decides whether to allow or block them. It is a fundamental method for controlling network access and implementing security policies.

Port Forwarding

A technique that redirects traffic from one IP address and port number to another, allowing external devices to access services on an internal network. Port forwarding is used to host servers (such as web servers) within a private network behind a router or firewall.

Stateful Inspection

A firewall feature that monitors the state of active connections and determines whether incoming packets are part of an existing, legitimate connection. It improves security by allowing the firewall to filter traffic more intelligently compared to basic packet filtering.

VPN (Virtual Private Network)

A secure encrypted connection over a public network (like the Internet) that allows remote users to access private networks securely. VPNs are widely used by organizations to provide remote workers with access to corporate networks.

IPsec (Internet Protocol Security)

A protocol suite used to secure IP communications by authenticating and encrypting each IP packet. IPsec is often used in VPNs to ensure secure communication over potentially insecure networks.

Rate Limiting

A technique **to restrict the number** of requests a user, application, or service can make to a server within a specific time period. It helps prevent server overload, abuse, or brute-force attacks.

Zero Trust

A security model that assumes no trust between users, devices, or systems, regardless of whether they are inside or outside the network perimeter. Every access request must be authenticated and authorized before granting access to resources.

IDS (Intrusion Detection System)

A security tool that monitors network traffic for suspicious activity and potential threats. IDS alerts administrators when a potential breach or attack is detected, but does not actively block or prevent attacks.

IPS (Intrusion Prevention System)

An extension of IDS, the Intrusion Prevention System not only detects but also blocks malicious traffic in real-time. It actively prevents detected attacks from succeeding by taking automatic actions.

DMZ (Demilitarized Zone)

A portion of a network that is exposed to the public, typically housing servers like web and email servers that must be accessible from the Internet. The DMZ is separated from the internal network to provide an additional layer of security.

Proxy Server

An intermediary server that acts as a gateway between users and the internet. A proxy can filter traffic, cache content, and improve privacy by masking users' IP addresses.

Firewall

A network security device that monitors and controls incoming and outgoing traffic based on predefined security rules. Firewalls can be hardware-based, software-based, or a combination of both, and they form the first line of defense in network security.

LAN (Local Area Network)

A network that connects devices within a small geographic area, such as a home, office, or campus. LANs enable devices to share resources like files, printers, and internet connections.

WAN (Wide Area Network)

A network that covers a large geographic area, connecting multiple LANs together. The Internet is the largest example of a WAN.

DNS (Domain Name System)

A hierarchical system that translates human-readable domain names (e.g., www.example.com) into IP addresses that computers use to identify each other on the network. DNS is essential for navigating the web.

ICMP (Internet Control Message Protocol)

A protocol used for diagnosing network issues and for error messages. Common ICMP tools include ping and traceroute, which test the reachability of hosts and network path latency.

IPv4 (Internet Protocol version 4)

The fourth version of the Internet Protocol, IPv4 provides an addressing scheme for identifying devices on a network using a 32-bit address format (e.g., 192.168.1.1). Due to address exhaustion, it is gradually being replaced by IPv6.

IPv6 (Internet Protocol version 6)

The most recent version of the Internet Protocol, IPv6 uses a 128-bit addressing scheme, allowing for a virtually unlimited number of unique IP addresses. It is designed to replace IPv4 due to the growing number of internet-connected devices.

SSH (Secure Shell)

A protocol that provides **a secure channel** over an unsecured network by using encryption. SSH is commonly used for remote management of systems, allowing secure login and command execution on remote machines.

TLS/SSL (Transport Layer Security / Secure Sockets Layer)

Protocols that provide encryption for data transmission over networks. SSL (now deprecated) and TLS are commonly used to secure web traffic, ensuring that sensitive information like login credentials and payment data are protected.

VLAN (Virtual Local Area Network)

A network configuration that allows you to segment a physical network into multiple logical networks. VLANs improve network performance and security by isolating network segments from each other while sharing the same physical hardware.

SYN Flood

A type of DDoS attack where attackers send a large number of SYN (synchronize) requests to a server, overwhelming its resources and preventing it from processing legitimate connection requests.

MTU (Maximum Transmission Unit)

The largest size of a packet that can be transmitted over a network. MTU settings can affect performance, as packets larger than the MTU are fragmented, which can lead to reduced efficiency.

Appendix F: Commonly Used Ports On Linux Servers

Linux servers often utilize a wide range of ports to facilitate various network services and applications. Each port is associated with a specific protocol or service, and understanding these ports is crucial for managing server security and functionality. Below is a list of commonly used ports on Linux servers, many of which can be controlled or restricted using Iptables or other firewall tools to allow or block traffic based on your server's needs.

20, 21 – FTP (File Transfer Protocol)
Port 21 is used for FTP commands.
Port 20 is used for FTP data transfer.

22 – SSH (Secure Shell)
Used for remote login and secure file transfers (e.g., scp, sftp).

25 – SMTP (Simple Mail Transfer Protocol)
Used for sending emails.

53 – DNS (Domain Name System)
Used for domain name resolution.

67, 68 – DHCP (Dynamic Host Configuration Protocol)
Used for dynamically assigning IP addresses to devices on a network.

80 – HTTP (HyperText Transfer Protocol)
Used for serving web pages over an unsecured connection.

110 – POP3 (Post Office Protocol)
Used for retrieving emails from a remote server.

123 – NTP (Network Time Protocol)
Used for clock synchronization between computer systems.

143 – IMAP (Internet Message Access Protocol)
Used for accessing emails on a remote server.

443 – HTTPS (HyperText Transfer Protocol Secure)
Used for serving web pages over a secure, encrypted connection (SSL/TLS).

465 – SMTPS (SMTP Secure)
Used for sending emails securely over SSL/TLS.

993 – IMAPS (IMAP Secure)
Secure version of IMAP, encrypted with SSL/TLS.

995 – POP3S (POP3 Secure)
Secure version of POP3, encrypted with SSL/TLS.

3306 – MySQL/MariaDB
Used for database connections to MySQL or MariaDB databases.

5432 – PostgreSQL
Used for database connections to PostgreSQL databases.

6379 – Redis
Used for in-memory database and caching service.

8080 – Alternative HTTP
Often used as an alternative port for HTTP web traffic.

8443 – Alternative HTTPS
Often used as an alternative port for HTTPS web traffic (secure).

10000 – Webmin
Used for web-based administration of Unix/Linux systems.

3000, 5000 – Custom Application Ports
Commonly used for custom web applications and development servers.

Additional Common Ports:

5900 – VNC (Virtual Network Computing) (used for remote desktop access).

25, 587 – SMTP (often 587 is used for secure email submission with STARTTLS).

993, 995 – IMAP/POP3 Secure (used for secure email retrieval).

Ports for Video and Audio Streaming

1935 – RTMP (Real-Time Messaging Protocol)
RTMP is a common protocol used for streaming audio, video, and data over the Internet. It is widely used for live streaming and is supported by platforms like YouTube, Twitch, and Facebook Live.

554 – RTSP (Real-Time Streaming Protocol)
RTSP is used for establishing and controlling media sessions between endpoints. It's a control protocol designed for real-time media streaming.

8554 – RTSP Alternative
Some RTSP implementations use port 8554 instead of 554 to avoid conflicts with other services.

8000, 8001 – Shoutcast/Icecast
These ports are often used for audio streaming by Shoutcast and Icecast servers. Icecast is commonly used for Internet radio.

1755 – MMS (Microsoft Media Server Protocol)
MMS is an older streaming protocol used primarily for streaming audio and video from Windows Media servers.

5004, 5005 – RTP (Real-Time Transport Protocol)
RTP is used for delivering audio and video over IP networks. It's often used in conjunction with RTSP for streaming and VoIP (Voice over IP) services.

8800 – HTTP Live Streaming (HLS)
HLS is a media streaming protocol used to deliver live and on-demand content over HTTP. Although it primarily uses HTTP ports (80 and 443), some custom implementations may use port 8800 or similar.

8080 – Alternative HTTP Streaming
Some services use port 8080 for HTTP-based streaming as an alternative to the standard port 80.

10000 – WebRTC (Web Real-Time Communication)
WebRTC allows for audio, video, and data sharing directly between browsers without needing plugins. It uses a range of dynamic ports, often starting at port 10000 (UDP) for interactive media sessions.

6970-6999 – QuickTime Streaming Server (QTSS)
QuickTime uses these ports for audio and video streaming.

3478-3481 – STUN/TURN (Session Traversal Utilities for NAT)
STUN and TURN are protocols used to traverse NAT (Network Address Translation) and allow peer-to-peer communication, often used in video conferencing and VoIP services.

Other Ports Relevant to Media Streaming

80, 443 – HTTP/HTTPS
Streaming services that use HTTP-based protocols (like HLS or DASH) for streaming often use the standard HTTP (80) or HTTPS (443) ports.

53 – DNS (Domain Name System)
Though not specific to streaming, DNS is essential for resolving domain names to IP addresses before accessing streaming services.

19302-19309 – Google STUN Servers (WebRTC)

These ports are used for WebRTC peer-to-peer connections, including audio and video calls.

10000-20000 (UDP) – VoIP and Streaming Ports
For VoIP and real-time video/audio streaming, UDP ports within this range are often used. Many streaming protocols dynamically assign UDP ports within this range.

Printer Ports:

515 – LPD/LPR (Line Printer Daemon)
A legacy protocol used for network printing. Commonly used on Unix/Linux systems to queue and send print jobs to networked printers.

631 – IPP (Internet Printing Protocol)
IPP is the default protocol used by modern printers and CUPS (Common Unix Printing System). It allows for printing, managing jobs, and querying printer status over a network.

9100 – RAW Port for Printing (JetDirect/RAW)
Used by many network printers (especially HP printers) for direct (RAW) printing. Often called the JetDirect protocol.

137-139, 445 – SMB/CIFS (Samba Printing)
Used for Windows file and print sharing over a network. If your Linux system is set up with Samba to allow printing via SMB, it will use these ports for communication.

Ports for Ham Radio Servers

EchoLink (VoIP for ham radio)
UDP 5198-5199: Used for voice communication.
TCP 5200: Used for connection to the EchoLink directory.

AllStarLink (Radio-over-IP for linking repeaters)
UDP 4569: AllStarLink protocol for VoIP-based communication.

D-STAR (Digital Smart Technologies for Amateur Radio)
UDP 20000-20010: Used for D-STAR repeater links and communication.

DMR (Digital Mobile Radio)
UDP 62031: Used for DMR gateways and communication between repeaters and hotspots.

Ports for Minecraft Servers

Java Edition (default port):
TCP 25565: The default port for Minecraft Java Edition. If you're hosting a Java server, this is the port that needs to be open.

Bedrock Edition (default port):
UDP 19132: The default port for Minecraft Bedrock Edition, used for both internal and external connections.

Special/Reserved Ports:

1–1023 – System Ports (privileged ports, used by well-known services).

1024–49151 – User Ports (registered for user services and applications).

49152–65535 – Dynamic/Private Ports (typically used for client-side ephemeral ports during communication).